Broccoli

Silence

RULES OF THUMB

RULES OF THUMB

73 authors reveal their fiction writing fixations

EDITED BY MICHAEL MARTONE AND SUSAN NEVILLE

WRITER'S DIGEST BOOKS

CINCINNATI, OHIO
www.writersdigest.com

EDITED BY *Jane Friedman*

DESIGNED BY *Grace Ring*

PRODUCTION COORDINATED
BY *Robin Richie*

10 09 08 07 06   5 4 3 2 1

Distributed in Canada by Fraser Direct, 100 Armstrong Avenue, Georgetown, ON, Canada L7G 5S4, Tel: (905) 877-4411. Distributed in the U.K. and Europe by David & Charles, Brunel House, Newton Abbot, Devon, TQ12 4PU, England, Tel: (+44) 1626 323200, Fax: (+44) 1626 323319, E-mail: mail@davidandcharles.co.uk. Distributed in Australia by Capricorn Link, P.O. Box 704, Windsor, NSW 2756 Australia, Tel: (02) 4577-3555.

Library of Congress Cataloging-in-Publication Data
Rules of thumb : 73 authors reveal their fiction writing fixations / edited by Michael Martone and Susan Neville.
    p. cm.
Includes index.
ISBN-13: 978-1-58297-391-3 (alk. paper)   ISBN-10: 1-58297-391-1
1. Fiction--Authorship. I. Martone, Michael. II. Neville, Susan.
PN3355.R86 2006   2005031953
808.3--dc22

fw
F+W PUBLICATIONS, INC.

ACKNOWLEDGMENT

I would like to thank Susan Neville for setting me straight and coming up with idea after idea when it to came collecting this catalog of advice. I must thank all my teachers especially Margaret Wiggs, John Sawyer, Kathy Neuhaus, James Lewinsky, Richard Cassell, and Robert Novak and all the writers who contributed here. And thank you to Jane Friedman and team F+W for measuring twice and cutting once. Everybody, cross your fingers.

Dedication

for Blanche Payne who taught me the difference

between a smidgen and a dash, a pinch and a tad

Table of Contents

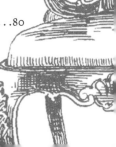

Four Finger Exercises and One for the Thumb: An Introduction

THUMB

When you have small hands and you want to play Rachmaninoff—whose fingers could span more than twenty keys—you end up having to roll the chords, rocking the hand from thumb to finger instead of playing each note simultaneously, the way Rachmaninoff wrote them.

This is true unless you have a piano teacher who has you repeatedly place your thumb on, say, middle C, and stretch the webbing between thumb and index finger, then between index finger and the middle and so forth, until, by the daily then yearly exercise of stretching, the fingers miraculously increase their span and you can reach higher up the keyboard, high enough to play the chord as Rachmaninoff heard it in his head when he composed it.

And so, in writing, there are things you hear, places you want to reach—not Rachmaninoff of course—but something vaguely Chekhovian perhaps, or Lawrentian or Dickensian or Catheresque—yet distinctly you. And you've thought often that if only there were rules of thumb, some secret exercises like that stretching of the hand in piano, that those rules might help you reach the places on the keyboard you can't quite seem to get to. And so, the genesis of *Rules of Thumb*.

MIDDLE

Didn't a very earnest Ernest Hemingway say over and over that to talk about something was to kill it? And yet he talked about it endlessly and in great detail. His prohibitions of adverbs. The sharpening of

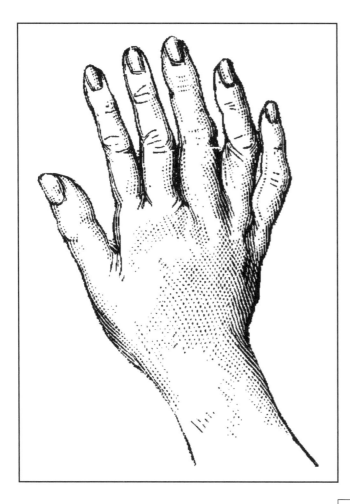

his pencils. The insider tip that one always know what comes next before stopping for the day, so as to have something to start with on the next. Thank Hemingway for the script, the setting, and the choreography, producing the whole public performance of the writer writing in the bloody bullring of the sidewalk café, the coffee shop, any clean, well-lighted place in the storm.

His interview with *The Paris Review* defined that genre and standardized the questions as to ritualistic warm-ups, superstitious tics, and fetishistic habits of crafting and composing. And in the opening of *A Movable Feast*, a book-length

riot of policy and procedure, Ernest provides way too much information as to how the apparatus of composition is intimately linked to visual stimulation, erectile function, and the seemingly effortless flow of a seductive narrative.

In spite of this, the big admonition persists: To talk about something kills it. When asked to contribute to *Rules of Thumb*, the novelist T.R. Pearson wrote, demurring, that the secret to writing is to sit down and write, and that was all he had to say on the subject. Writers write. But writers more often than not are not writing. They are waiting to write, preparing to write, rehearsing, practicing, taking notes, outlining, reading. On top of the anxiety of writing (or not writing) is this other anxiety—that all the activities of the prelude, in reality, are not prelude at all, but a symphony of fiddling around, a divertimento of tuning up.

INDEX

We asked nearly one hundred writers to contribute very brief essays on rules of thumb they use when composing prose. The authors in their essays were to choose a rule and then expand it briefly and (we hoped) with wit, authority, and precision. The rule might be the simplest of prohibitions—don't use too many adjectives, or only use "said" for attributions—or positive exhortations—write what you know, or show, don't tell. Some essays (we believed; we hoped again) might be revelatory and personal, confessions of an individual author's phobias, superstitions, spells, compulsions, habits. We added in our solicitation that the more eccentric, idiosyncratic, or grumpy the essay, the better. In this manner, we theorized, the book would be a rich collection of succinct, useful tips for writers at all levels, advice at once memorable and easily referable, entertaining and thought provoking.

We also expected, with the number of contributors, that some of the advice would be contradictory, at odds with other essays in the book and maybe even at odds within itself. Conflicts would add to the book's charm as readers negotiated the opposing arguments passionately and confidently rendered. Adding to that charm would be the underlying sense that these essays, written by some of the finest prose stylists working today, are in a way a confessional—a chance to hear a secret, uncover

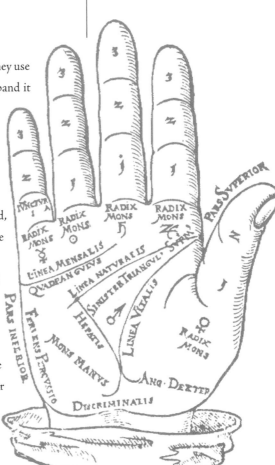

a fetish, or discover a lucky ritual or habitual gesture held dearly and practiced religiously by an individual contributor.

Many writers told us as they took up the task that they found such existential confrontations with such deeply held opinions illuminating, surprising, and, well, refreshing. Many had been doing something without thinking why they did for years. Innocently, they worked on their essays only to discover that a simmering scold from a teacher long ago had lodged in a crevice of memory, or a tossed-off bit of advice delivered by a workshop critic in college had stuck and stayed at hand. They discovered their patterns, their wiring, and their rewiring. They made themselves conscious of the unconscious, of the patterning of patterns naturalized and internalized long ago.

PINKY

We expected the essays would, in their very composition, enact the rule of thumb being written about, and many do. We also asked that each author consider including in the essay an example of "good" or "bad" use of the rule under consideration. The aggregate of this collection then is that it has become a lively symposium on style as well as a useful reference manual of the various mechanical and inspirational components of composition.

RING

Many writers pointed out to us the derivation of the phrase rule of thumb, tracing it back to the handy and literal gauge once used in the measuring of a stick for beating: The rule of thumb for the size of a proper switch was the diameter of a thumb. The roots of the phrase rest in a very real application of discipline. Our little experiment, presented here, also is about discipline—discipline not in the sense of punishment, but in the sense of a defined branch of knowledge—the nominative, not the predicate. A discipline.

Writers impose upon themselves various limitations, boundaries, restrictions, and rules in order to better define for themselves what it is exactly they are doing. They define by definition. It gives them something to push against, something to solve, something to struggle with. And as many of the writers represented here suggest, a clear understanding and mastery of the rules (any rules in a storm) is often the essential first step to bending and breaking them. The end desired, of course, is to transcend the arbitrary rules altogether and thereby establish a whole new set of parameters to frame and define the enterprise of making meaning. The rules aren't so much a whip to abrade but an accelerator, a cracking whip that can snap us into a new dimension: a new realm made possible by the mastery of what, like the mysterious resonance of the chord played whole, was originally only imagined. ❧

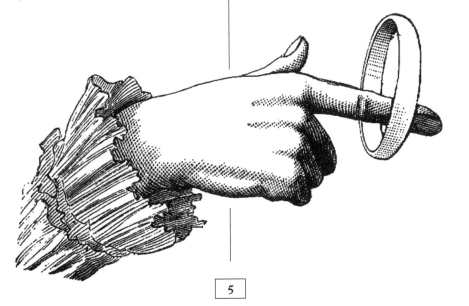

The Ink-Stained Thumb

by John Barth

Thumb-rule number one for aspiring writers, it goes without saying, is: Be wary of writers' rules of thumb. Anton Chekhov liked the smell of rotting apples in his writing desk. Edna Ferber advised nothing more interesting on that desk's far side than a blank wall. Ernest Hemingway and Scheherazade, for different reasons, liked to close their day's (or night's) output in midstory, even in midsentence. I myself advise no more than that you merely perpend such advisements and predilections, including mine to follow, en route to discovering by hunch, feel, trial, and error what best floats your particular boat. Too many rules of thumb can make a chap all thumbs.

That said, I report that, for this writer at least, *regularity* is as helpful with the muse as with the bowels: a comparison to be taken just so far and no further. Go to your worktable at the same time daily, establish

your personal prep routine, and you're likely to find that, just as making breakfast (to change analogies) may sharpen your appetite, so some established little ritual of muse-invocation may get your creative juices flowing. After the breakfast afore alluded to with wife and newspaper, followed by that *toilette* likewise alluded to, and ten-minute routine of stretching exercises picked up half a century ago from an RCAF training manual, I refill my thermal coffee mug and disappear into my scriptorium no later than half past eight every weekday morning. It has separate workspaces for creation, production, and business; ignoring the third of those (appointments calendar, file drawers, check registers and accounting ledgers, telephone, clock, and calculator, all relegated to *later*), I pause at the second just long enough to boot up and then promptly anesthetize my more-or-less-trusty Macintosh, which will remain in standby mode unless this morning's work is to be the revision and editing of an already first-drafted text—for me, the most enjoyable stage of writing, because it *feels* agreeably creative but is so much easier than invention and composition. Turning then to the *sanctum sanctorum*, the worktable consecrated to composition, I do the following routine preps, the musely equivalent of those earlier RCAF exercises.

1. Insert a set of Mack's earplugs from supply in worktable drawer: a habit carried over from half a century ago when my now middle-aged children were high-energy tots and their father was an overworked, underpaid young college instructor obliged to snatch the odd hour of writing time at a little desk in the bedroom. By the time the nest was empty and my work area a more commodious and quiet personal space, the earplug habit was as fixed as Chekhov's requisite rotting apples. My muse sings only through ambient silence—her song not always clearly distinguishable, I confess, from the tinnitus familiar to many of us oldsters.

2. Ears plugged, slide selfward the worn, stained, and battered three-ring loose-leaf binder procured during freshman orientation week at Johns Hopkins in 1947, in which has been first-drafted every page of my fiction since those green undergraduate days. It's as weathered now as its owner, who, however, counts on its continuing to hang together for at least as long as he does.

3. Open that "serviceable old thing" (as W.H. Auden fondly addressed his aging body) either to the page in progress or to the blank next thing, and take from its nestling-place among the gently rusting triple rings the somewhat less venerable—but by me equally venerated—Parker 51 fountain pen bought forty-plus years ago in Mr. Pumblechook's premises in Rochester,

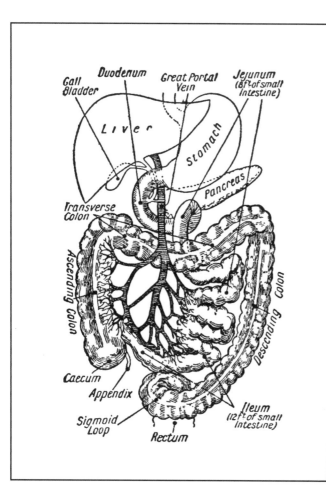

Duodenum

Gall Bladder

Great Portal Vein

Jejunum (8ft of small intestine)

L i v e r

Stomach

Pancreas

Transverse Colon

Ascending Colon

Descending Colon

Caecum

Appendix

Ileum (12ft of small intestine)

Sigmoid Loop

Rectum

Regularity is as helpful with the muse as with the bowels: a comparison to be taken just so far and no further.

England, in honor of the great Boz. Uncap and fill that instrument with its daily draught of Permanent Jet Black Quink, and then. …

Well, that depends. Like Hemingway and company aforementioned, I try to end each morn's first-drafting while the going's good, with maybe a brief penciled or ballpointed note of what's to follow (the Parker is reserved strictly for first-draft composition, not for notes, correspondence, and suchlike mundanities). If today's session involves work in progress, then reviewing and editing the printout of yesterday's installment usually suffices to reorient the imagination and pump the creative adrenaline enough for me to resume what Anne Tyler has felicitously called "the muscular cursive" of penmanship—which a couple of hours later I'll break off in mid-whatever, date in parentheses (with ballpoint pickup note appended), and type into the waiting word processor for ease of subsequent revision, already editing the draft as I transcribe it. If on the other hand what awaited me back there at 8:30 was the between-projects three-hole ruled blank page, it's a whole 'nother story, so to speak: one in which I'm likely to have recapped and renestled that refilled Parker, taken up Papermate and clipboard instead, and scratched hopefully preliminary notes toward … who knows what? Maybe a mini essay on writerly rules of thumb?

Most prose writers nowadays in every genre—perhaps most *poets*, even—dispense altogether with the venerable—to them perhaps obsolete—medium of longhand and compose directly on the PC. For all I know, maybe even their preliminary note-making is done on laptop or Palm Pilot. If so, so be it: As afore declared, whatever floats the old boat. For yours truly, however, the equation of narrative flow with the literal flow of ink onto paper, of the fountain pen with the fount of inspiration, holds as firmly as my right hand holds that maroon-and-brushed-silver Parker 51: a rule of (sometimes ink-stained) thumb. 🐛

John Barth

Novelist, short-story writer, and essayist John Barth is a Professor Emeritus in The Writing Seminars of Johns Hopkins University. He is known for the postmodernist and metafictive quality of his work and for 800-page novels like *The Sot-Weed Factor*.

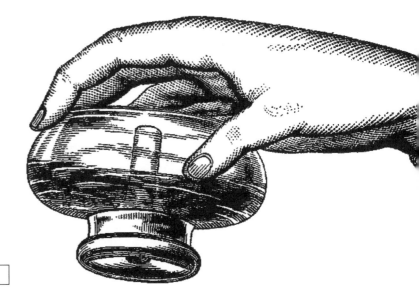

Using Words With Musical Precision

by Barbara Shoup

1984: Indiana University Writers' Conference. I'm sitting in a cluttered hotel room in the Memorial Union, where I've come for the personal critique of my manuscript by the novelist teaching the workshop I'm attending—a woman in her fifties, the author of wry, elegant novels about the complexities of family life. She holds my novel excerpt in her hands, shuffles through it, and I strain—as subtly as I can—to see if there are many comments on the pages. I can't see any at all.

This could be a good sign: *It's perfect! What's to say?* Or a bad sign: *It's dreadful! What's to say?* Maybe it's no sign at all. She's been battling cancer, I've heard. Maybe she just doesn't have the energy for anybody's writing but her own. She does look awfully tired. During our workshop sessions, she often sits quietly at the head of the table observing us as if we might be akin to one of the dysfunctional families in her novels.

She's observing me right now, with a cool gaze, and when, finally, she speaks, it is in reference to a single word circled in red pen on a page in the middle of the manuscript. "This," she says, pointing to it, then thumbing through to where the same word is circled on a later page, "is the kind of word that you should never allow yourself to use more than once in a book." For the life of me, I cannot remember what the word was. Nor can I remember what else—if anything—she said to me that day. Just that I thought, *What?*

The remark seemed like nitpicking to me, absurd. But she was right! Whatever the word was, it was clear to me once I thought about it that, indeed, it should only be used once in a book. I

> *I understood that it was not so much about any single word but about the kind of close attention a serious writer pays to her work.*

couldn't have explained why. I still can't. Nor could I create a list of words to which the novelist's rule would always apply. Nonetheless, the rule turned out to be one I've lived by—and, in time, I understood that it was not so much about any single word but about the kind of close attention a serious writer pays to her work.

A novel is not unlike a musical composition in its effect: each word like a music note used with a particular intention. Listen to Barber's Adagio for Strings, which makes brilliant musical use of this rule. Then listen to, say, Barry Manilow, and you'll hear the difference. 🐇

Barbara Shoup

Barbara Shoup is the author of five novels and a nonfiction book co-authored with Margaret-Love Denman, *Novel Ideas: Contemporary Authors Share the Creative Process*. Her short fiction, poetry, essays, and interviews have appeared in *The Louisville Review*, *Persuasions: The Jane Austen Journal*, *Rhino*, *The New York Times*, and *The Writer*, among others.

Complexity

by Paul Maliszewski

I told the student she should revive the philandering husband. When her story opens, he's in the hospital, in a coma, the victim of a car crash. His wife remains at his side, watching over him and keeping quiet vigil. Inside, however, she's fuming. Her husband has spoken only once during his coma, coming to consciousness just long enough to mutter the name of his mistress—Maria. Otherwise, he does not move or feel. He cannot communicate.

"Why not," I asked, "bring this husband back to life?"

The story was melodramatic, sure, the very ingredients soap operas are confected from, but the student did have two characters, each interesting enough. It's just that nothing ever happened between them—because nothing really could. Instead, the wife bides her time, remembering the past, the personal history she shares with her husband, and their relationship—which had, of course, been souring. She remembers also the night she received that fateful phone call from the police, saying her husband was in an accident. She rushed to the scene, just as her husband and a woman—Maria—are pulled from the crumpled car. Her husband's in a tux. Squad cars are all around, their lights flashing. Maria's in a dress—a fancy, sequined number. The wife grieves. She feels sorrow. The first pains of possible loss grip her stomach and then twist. Days later, while she waits in the hospital room, her memory of the tux and that dress bother her. The dress, in particular—so ostentatious, so red—eats at her.

The main problem I saw was that the wife has nobody to express these thoughts to. No friend or doctor, no sympathetic nurse. She could only carry on long hypothetical arguments with her husband, addressing herself to his inert body. She imagines what he might say if only he were awake.

"Why not," I asked, "make their arguments real?"

Much of the mess of these characters' lives—and the complexity of the student's story—was held at bay and kept safely outside the boundaries of the narrative by a contrivance of the plot: The husband could not awake. The characters had so much to discuss, though, so much yelling to do, so many arguments to air and so many opportunities for quick cuts, repressed emotions, and sudden outbursts. I felt sure there would be in their future surprising reminders of that night, the tux, and the sequined dress. Yet none of this could happen, because the wife stayed entirely in her head. The story itself was in a coma. It was static, without event.

I had seen stories like this before. That fall was the semester of the comatose narrative. An embittered stand-up comedian in another story, a man without luck or any prospects of sitcom stardom, returns to his hometown for a performance at the bar where he began his career. But again, nothing happens. In fact, that night's performance was like any other: not funny. Nobody he knows shows up, and the comedian cannot even muster the curiosity required to leave the bar, go outside, and see the town where he once lived.

In a third story, called "Ten Minutes," a woman awaits the results of her pregnancy test. The story ends when her wait is over. No results, no ramifications. The student had told a lively but mostly hypo-

thetical story about what the woman might say or do and, in turn, what she supposes her parents, her friend, and the guy she liked, sort of, might say or do back to her. As with the other stories, however, this one offered only an interior view, with the most dramatic episode—the messy life that must follow the results—left unwritten and unimagined.

That was the fall, too, of a graduation story in which the main character, an older sister, returns home to see her younger brother graduate from high school. She's a bit estranged from her parents, it turns out, and her brother was, when younger, thoughtless and prone

I resolved to face the moment of greatest complexity in a story—in every story—and write in its direction, not straying or shying away until I reached it.

to violent outbursts. Unfortunately, she never gets to the ceremony. The character, like the story, is stuck in traffic, inching forward and then stopping.

Several characters that semester sought to escape their stories, choosing to flee from some dramatic episode, a confrontation, or a spot of emotional stickiness. They ran away in the literal sense. One character just disappeared into the woods. Her

footprints were covered by snow so not even readers could follow. Other characters took metaphorical flight. They avoided and evaded and shirked. In still another story, a hairdresser and her wealthy client keep a regular Saturday appointment for several years running but never actually speak to one another. The hairdresser has ideas about her client—where her money comes from and how she behaves, for starters—but she never ventures anything more expressive than a curt "good morning." Scissor snips pass between them, but little else. What can happen when an author allows nothing to occur? Another character, perhaps expressing best the entire workshop's severe allergy to event and significance, stepped into the street at what would become the abrupt end of his story and was—that's right—struck by an oncoming car.

My students seemed to consider plot not a series of events that happen in a story, but instead a series of obstacles that, ideally, should keep anything from developing. Their plots conspired openly, brazenly even, as if the authors were allied against their own characters. Their plots held off all consequences—and all significance. I pictured barricades along the front lines of a protest, mounted police, cops in riot gear armed with nightsticks and Plexiglas shields. These plots had no intention of backing down. After all, they had the force of reality on their side. As several students pointed out, sometimes patients can stay in comas for months, even years. What's more, everybody knows how traffic going to these big graduations turns into knots. It's always bumper to bumper.

But I held my ground. I spoke to the class not as a longtime advocate of meaty, action-driven plots or of stories that embrace complexity and give form to life's big mess. I spoke rather as one who had once suffered a similar allergic reaction to significance. I had avoided consequence. In story after story, I dodged important encounters. For instance, I didn't allow myself to write about love—even the word itself was *verboten*, embargoed by strict customs agents in my direct employ—not because I lacked the feelings, but because I thought I'd be unable to write about them any way but adequately. What's worse, the feelings, I thought, would overwhelm my stories, like waves flipping over tiny canoes and rafts lashed together from small trees. At the time, I was happy if my stories merely floated along, getting from start to finish. I saw no purpose in testing their hardiness with storms.

I created my characters then not from memory, out of the material given me by my life, but from whole cloth. To do otherwise—to make "grandma" at all resemble my grandmother, even if only in passing—meant I would have to, when I was done writing, reconcile the shortcomings of my character (feeble, incomplete) alongside the living subject's grandness. If the portrait came out looking unrecognizable, a hash of timid descriptions, mechanical gestures, and wooden dialogue, what might the subject think? And what might my grandmother think of me? Even if I didn't show her—and I showed everyone almost nothing then—I still knew well enough how great the gap was between what I observed and what I made. I judged myself and could all too easily take the measure of my many failures.

Much later—and I recall this process taking several years, at least—I resolved to face the moment of greatest complexity in a story—in every story—and write in its direction, not straying or shying away until I reached it. I did not think myself a better writer necessarily, or even up to the task. I suppose I had merely become less afraid of the results being quite poor. So here and there I used the word *love*. And I addressed myself to the mess of life. I treated it as blessed, in fact, and something to be grateful for. In time, slowly at first, I saw and recognized some telling little pieces—a friend's way of smiling, say, when ashamed; or an uncle repeatedly correcting my mother for saying *choicey*, instead of *choosey*; my father's arms crossed across an old white T-shirt, his heavy parka blackened around the neckline; and one morning, while I was visiting cousins, when I awoke to find my eyes sealed shut with sleep—all those stray bits, all that life, that I managed somehow to get down all right. ❧

Paul Maliszewski

An experienced writing teacher who lives and works in Washington, DC, Paul Maliszewski has recently published articles and stories in *Harper's*, *Smithsonian*, *Granta*, *Oxford American*, *McSweeney's*, *The Paris Review*, and *The Wilson Quarterly*. His stories have been awarded two Pushcart Prizes, and he has edited four collections of writing, including *Paper Placemats*, an anthology of writing and artwork about the significance of place.

Broccoli

You Must Eat Broccoli Before You Begin

by M.T. Anderson

You must eat broccoli before you begin. Broccoli contains formidable doses of vitamin A, vitamin C, folic acid, calcium, iron, potassium, and beta-carotene. The vitamin C facilitates the easy absorption of the iron. The phytochemicals incite detoxifying enzyme production.

I find the taste repellent, greening and graying as one moves from stalk to floret. The flavor alters with density, age, pesticide, and packaging, sometimes recalling a clogged, black mountain tarn, or mulch, or plastic pellets, or (at best) the loam of the good road. Nonetheless, you should eat it, because it confers an almost supernatural clarity of thought and engagement with the senses.

My metabolism is rapacious, subjecting me to successive phases of enervation in which I can barely remember common conjunctions or the names of people I've known for years. Broccoli, taken about an hour before I begin writing, reverses this process. Abruptly, the mind is Olympian, the eyes uncross, the hand is sure.

The vegetable's name in Italian means "little, well-muscled arm"; Romans called it the five green fingers of Jupiter.

Drusus, son of the Roman emperor Tiberius, abjured all other foods and ate only broccoli for a year. His urine became bright green.

The vegetable's name in Italian means "little, well-muscled arm"; Romans called it the five green fingers of Jupiter.

We should eat it for the clarity, but also because in its form it ramifies, and so reminds us of causality. We should eat it because it is cruciferous, and we all have our little rood to carry. What better thing for an author, godlike, to ingest than a miniature tree? If only, before every stint of writing, we devoured not simply this tiny woodland but also diminutive houses, little lawns, trinket people, taking them all within us, holding landscapes and continents in acid, observed by the stomach, applauded by the intestines—and ushered thence to their final glory, their new form, their reemancipation.

(Best steamed; serve with lemon or butter.) 🌱

M.T. Anderson

M.T. Anderson is fiction editor for *3rd Bed*. His novel *Feed* was a finalist for the National Book Award and the *Boston Globe*–Horn Book Award, and was awarded a *Los Angeles Times* Book Prize. He is currently on the faculty of Vermont College's MFA in Writing for Children & Young Adults Program.

Plankland Rules

by Kate Bernheimer

In nursery school I was blessed with a best friend, Diana Selig, with whom I shared a passionate love for imaginary rules. At Green Acres Nursery School, before our naps—to be taken on green, shiny mats laid out neatly in rows of five children in the cool basement of a rambling farmhouse—we'd play Kiss, Hug, and Fall Down. This meant kissing each other's cheeks, one-by-one, hugging, turning around three times, and falling into a heap. We allowed Julie Braham to participate, needing the game to have three participants to work, to put us properly to sleep. We had our mothers write down the rules of Kiss, Hug, and Fall Down on pieces of paper that we folded up into tiny pieces and stored in our pockets, lest they fall into the wrong hands.

A few years later, in second and third Grade, Diana and I shared a teacher and classroom; the school was experimenting with combining ages. We had a notebook in which we inscribed, secretly, Rules of Second-and-Third:

1. We do not like Mrs. Johnston (our teacher, with whom we were actually enamored), so do not smile at her.

2. Hide in tires at recess (a new playground had been installed with giant tires incorporated; they provided good shelter from bullies, who made frightening passes at little girls with glasses).

3. Do not let anyone else EVER see these rules. Unfortunately, the small notebook—which one of our mothers had gotten for free at a Hallmark Store and given to her "young authors," as we were called—was discovered by none other than Mrs. Johnston herself. Though we had written the rules in an elaborate code involving cursive letters and cursive numbers (which we'd invented), we had, unfortunately,

inscribed the Code Rules in the notebook's first pages. There we also featured the names of various flowers we liked—codes plus flowers, this made perfect sense to us. Mrs. Johnston called us in one recess (having discovered us in our Top Secret Tire Location) and seemed to be crying, or so we remember. Mortified, we vowed never to write down our rules again—or, at least, to so foolishly reveal the code breaker.

Over the years we developed many such secrets, and to this day we both remember Plankland most vividly of all. Plankland was the imaginary village that existed between Beethoven Elementary School

and Diana's house, a three-story Victorian in which certain rules were in effect; in my parents' two-story Colonial, fewer rules seemed necessary. There, we were free to watch television, eat popcorn, carve pumpkins, and play mainly at being normal girls. In Plankland, one had to walk single file. In Plankland, one walked on planks suspended miles above the ground. If one stumbled—causing one not to fall but to instill fear in the other Plankgirl—one would be punished by Plankland's mistress, The Governess, who resided in the attic of 7 Ashmont Road. When we'd arrive at Diana's house, we'd scurry upstairs to mete out the punishment, which generally involved writing stories about Plankland on carbon copy paper. These stories were folded up tightly and secreted inside a cigar box we kept in a tiny closet under a dormer window.

"What are you girls playing up there?" Mrs. Selig—also known as Other Mother—would call up the stairs. "NOTHING," we'd yell back, hearts pounding. Nothing could be revealed. If we were discovered—if Plankland was discovered—we knew all would be lost. Just as our secret scribbles in that Hallmark notebook had led to the horrible devastation of Poor Mrs. Johnston, so too would Plankland cause vast demise.

It was the secret of writing, we knew.

Eventually, we grew up. We turned ten. We craved praise for our imaginative powers and began publishing a village newspaper: not a Plankland newspaper, of course, for Plankland was forever a secretive world, but *The Waban Bulletin*, a newspaper for real people who lived in our real town in Massachusetts. Within two years we had thirty subscribers, a bank account at Waban Bank, and several advertisers (including Colin Selig's Lawn Mowing Service and Art Moger's Jokes—my grandfather, who wrote pun books, would write a joke for hire, for a dollar, the ad proclaimed). The *Waban Bulletin* was public, very public indeed. Yet after each issue was printed—mimeographed at my father's office downtown—we'd put a sheet over the card table in the *Bulletin's* office, turn on a flashlight, and read it aloud to each other in private. KEEP OUT, shouted a sign on the office's doorway: EDITORS AT WORK.

Over the years I've been told many rules by authors I deeply admire:

♦ Never put a dream in a story because the only thing worse than being told someone's dream at a bar, over cocktails, is having to read about a character's dream in a piece of fiction.

♦ Never have a ship in a poem—it's been done too well already. But if you have to have a ship in a poem, never have another ship cross its path. Two ships crossing in the night? Ring a bell?

♦ If you write a long sentence, or if you have a sentence with long words in it which makes it a sort of long sentence too, always end that sentence with a nice, hard word, one that ends in a consonant.

♦ Don't leave any sentence in that makes you cringe.

Yet the only rule I can say with great confidence that I live by as a writer, I learned at Green Acres with my friend Diana: Keep it a secret. To this day, I write my novels in secret. Some would say this is a compulsion of mine. Of course, "secret" is different from "private." (*The Secret Garden*, one of my favorite books, was not, after all, called The Private Garden.) Privacy is more of a luxury, though it also is more democratic: you can have privacy in a library, a café, an attic, a bus. Secrecy, on the other hand, is secret. Secrecy means my husband asking, after two years of my not giving him a manuscript to read, "When are you going to start writing that second novel?" To that, I ran upstairs to my alcove, pulled 94 manuscript pages—for me, nearly the whole novel—out of a pale pink folder, and tripped over myself in wild zeal to shove the pages into his hands. "See? See? I have been writing! You just didn't know! I do it in secret!"

Childish, I know.

But secrecy means everything to me. For it reminds me of Plankland, and those blissful, treacherous walks home on planks, planks suspended high, high above this earth in a land we ourselves had discovered. Now, when I write novels and essays, I write them in secret, dreaming of Plankland Rules. ❧

Kate Bernheimer

Kate Bernheimer edited *Mirror Mirror on the Wall: Women Writers Explore Their Favorite Fairy Tales* and is the author of a novel, *The Complete Tales of Ketzia Gold*. She teaches at the University of Alabama.

A Primer on the Proper Use of Thumbs in the Revision Process

by Michael Wilkerson

My rule of thumb, unlike most of those in this volume, actually requires the usage of not one, but both thumbs. Holding them as clamps along with their respective index fingers, grip tightly on a piece of writing. Anything less than fifteen pages will do for most writers, though people with exceptionally strong hands might be able to perform this trick with up to twenty-five pages of normal-weight paper.

For best results, there should be about an inch of white space between the two thumbs. If the writer is right-handed, pull with the right thumb, ripping the paper vertically in half. If left-handed, ditto in the opposite way. Once satisfied, place ripped halves in trash. If adrenaline is still surging through the writer, stack halves, reposition thumbs on horizontal axis of paper, and tear again. Repeat until exhausted. Dispose of results. Recycling is considered virtuous and even-tempered.

> *As she converted my ripped half-pages into quarters, she said, "Your writing has no structure. Writing must be structured."*

This technique was taught to me after more than twenty years as a professional writer—for newspapers, universities, magazines, nonprofit organizations, for myself. There was a new boss in my office. It was a time of excitement and optimism. There would be fresh ideas, creativity all over the campus, and new appreciation for the art form at which I had been told I excelled—speechwriting. The university would reach new levels of excellence.

Maybe I would get a raise.

Oops.

Instead of offering me the reaction all writers believe they deserve—unconditional praise—the new boss instead fancied herself a teacher of the craft, from the Really Old School.

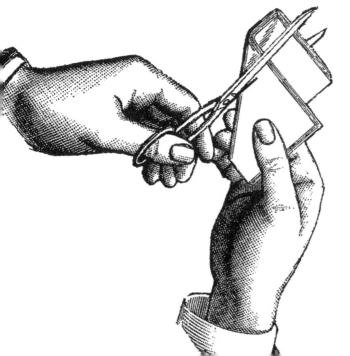

"Speeches should have a point," she said as she rejected my first submission and asked me to try again. On my second attempt, she demonstrated the thumb technique with my draft while stating, "Good writers always use an outline." As she converted my ripped half-pages into quarters, she said, "Your writing has no structure. Writing must be structured."

I was getting old. Forty-six. I knew now that I would never learn to write. So I found a different boss instead. When he wants me to prepare a speech, he asks me to take out a legal pad, and begins to dictate. "I already know what I want to say," he says. At last, I can rest my thumbs. ❧

Michael Wilkerson

Michael Wilkerson works downstairs at Indiana University, directly below the room where he was taught the Rules of Thumb that appear in this volume. He writes fiction and essays and has been the executive director of two artists' colonies.

Take That Job and Show It

by Alyce Miller

Characters in fiction need jobs. Just like their real-life counterparts, they need something to do besides sit around and worry about their troubles. Unless they're independently wealthy or landed gentry, they need some visible means of supporting their cramped, cold-water flats or spacious mansions, their substance abuse, their unhealthy habits, their existential crises, their dysfunctional families, their illicit pursuits, their wildest dreams, their doomed loves, and other self-destructive impulses. And by employment, I mean that fictional characters should be engaged in some occupation other than the two favored by student writers: (1) aspiring young writer, or (2) disaffected college student aspiring to be a writer.

Simply put, characters in fiction, just like the rest of us slogging it out in the real world, have to work. Even if what they do is illegal or immoral, they still have bills to pay and children to raise, and everyone needs to eat! Yet in much of the student fiction I read, characters often seem strangely jobless, moving through their fictional worlds weightless and unmoored. Even when an occupation is alluded to (Dan is a fireman, or Gertrude is a nurse), characters seem to never need to be at their workplace! The occupation, or at least the character's relationship to it, never gets developed. And relying on a few props, like a pair of fireman's boots in the closet or a stethoscope close at hand, doesn't convince anyone.

How characters spend their time—even outside of the story—frames time, event, and, ultimately, what lies at the heart of all fiction: a character's desire. Employment supplies contour and texture to the specifics of a character's life. Jobs of all stripes can add nuance and complication.

How characters spend their time—even outside of the story—frames time, event, and, ultimately, what lies at the heart of all fiction: a character's desire.

What's it like for this particular character to be a hotel clerk? To work in a slaughterhouse? To tend bar? To perform open-heart surgery? Does the character like or hate the job? Does the character wish he or she were doing something else and, if so, what? Is the character doing his or her dream job when—bam!—something happens? What are some of the tools of the trade? Does the character work at night or in the day? Are there co-workers? Does the character have other aspirations and passions competing for time and attention?

The conflict in a good deal of fiction is built, even if obliquely, around the notion of *occupation*. Even the privileged, over-indulged Scarlett O'Hara had a role; and then she had a reversal of fortune that forced her to resort to desperate measures to get ahold of cash. Why? Eventually even Miss Scarlett needed the bucks.

Occupations also give characters a reason to be or not to be at certain places at certain times. Even a character who is a drifter (Aunt Sylvie in *Housekeeping*) or a drunken profligate (Dmitri Karamazov in *The Brothers Karamazov*) still has an "occupation." And what about kid characters? Children are often industrious and invent ingenious ways to make a few bucks for the movies or designer clothing (even if it's mooching off their parents, or recycling bottles), or they might even have—heaven forbid!—household chores or schoolwork.

In some works of fiction, a character's job may take center stage, fomenting crucial conflicts and tensions. Take, for example, the multivalenced subtleties introduced with the married dentists in Jane Smiley's *The Age of Grief*, and the impact their shared profession has, in part, on the troubled couple as they confront a crisis in their marriage. What about the central role of Bartleby's tedious job as a scrivener in the short story by Melville? Or, in Richard Wright's *Native Son*, Bigger Thomas's job as chauffeur, a job that puts him in close proximity with Mary and makes possible the tragic misstep that eventually leads to her murder? How does, say, the very lack of broader occupational opportunity affect such literary characters as the unwed and pregnant Charity Royall from Edith Wharton's *Summer*? Or the itinerant farmhands Janie Crawford and Tea Cake in Zora Neale Hurston's *Their Eyes Were Watching God*? What about the conflict generated by occupation in J.M. Coetzee's bleak novel *Disgrace*, first in the indiscretions of Professor Lurie, who is dismissed after an affair with a female student, and later on, following his downfall, in his occupation euthanizing animals at a rural animal shelter?

Think how the mysterious past employment that gener-

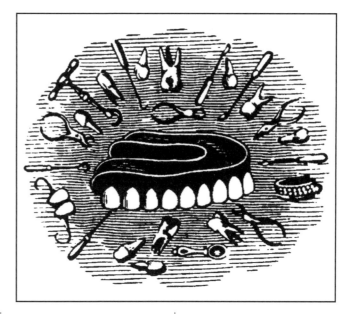

ated Jay Gatsby's leisure and wealth dominates *The Great Gatsby* and leads to all sorts of speculations by its characters, or how subtly the nymphet-obsessed scholar Humbert Humbert's past job as a perfume ad man infiltrates *Lolita* in small resonances.

Many friends from other countries have repeatedly told me that it is a very American habit to ask, when first meeting a stranger, *What do you do?* We size people up, evaluate them, make judgments and connections, based on their answer to this question. It may feel like a less intrusive way of locating or positioning people than saying *Who are you?* But that is, in effect, what the question signifies. By focusing on occupation, we begin to gain entrée to the person, to open that person up for discovery.

Used even peripherally in fiction, occupation adds dimension. Foregrounded through details, a character's job might even form the center of conflict.

Doctor, lawyer, tailor, knight, maid, filmmaker, detective, sailor, pilot, accountant, judge, tutor, mother, police officer, housewife, farmer, photographer, flight attendant, jeweler, plumber, secretary, teacher, overseer, painter, disc jockey, soldier, architect, postal worker, bus driver, gardener, cardsharp, news anchor, professor, musician, restaurant owner, hairdresser, retail clerk, drug dealer, prostitute, graduate student, dancer, hobo, plantation owner, scholar, scientist, slave, actress, junk collector, governess, babysitter, seamstress, athlete, and even a king or queen or two have all been represented in fiction.

Agrarian, industrial, technological, rural, urban, suburban—occupation is intimately connected with setting, and setting (physical, cultural, social, psychological) is where a character lives and breathes.

Even if the job is thankless or dead-end, temporary or illegal, or only marginally relevant to the story, attention to what a character does opens up a narrative arc. In the case of *The Accidental Tour-*

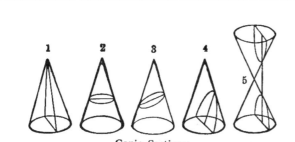

Conic Sections.

The two principal forms are fig. 5, giving the hyperbola, and fig. 3, giving the ellipse. Fig. 4 is the intermediate case, giving the parabola. The degenerate form of the hyperbola is a pair of straight lines, as shown in fig. 1. Fig. 2 shows the circle as a special case of the ellipse, in which the plane becomes perpendicular to the axis of the cone.

ist, Muriel's job as a dog trainer is key to the unfolding of central events and romance, while Joe Trace's peripherally mentioned occupation as a door-to-door cosmetics salesman in *Jazz* carries larger implications about deceit and "masking."

And even if a character is unemployed or retired, we need to know from what.

The glaring absence of such particulars about a character's occupation often leaves giant holes in fiction. The absence of income may raise serious doubts about how a character can afford to support extravagant tastes or just hang out all day with friends. Simply put, who's footing the bill?

So skip those dreadful character bios and résumés that have been so egregiously urged on young writers by advice-givers as a way to flesh out your characters. And forget those lethal character questionnaires: Does my character believe in God? (Yes or No) Does my character like fried chicken? (Yes or No) What's my character's favorite color—fuchsia or ecru? To find out who a character is, start to pay close attention to what the character does. Though characters presumably also brush and floss their teeth, take their cars to be repaired, come down with the flu, clean house, have sex, and pay taxes, the reader does not need to be privy to all details of quotidian life. But when a character is *occupied*, a fuller life is readily suggested. A character who has to be at the office or day-care center or school or store or research lab has a life. When characters get in or out of cars, walk through doors, or crawl in or out of bed, they move through three-dimensional space.

When the alarm clock goes off or a telephone rings, the character has to act. An employed character—whether it's a father rising early to transport a child to school, or a teenage girl heading off to clean a neighbor's house, or a corporate executive late to an important meeting—is already in motion. Another way to put it is that employed characters have purpose. And, besides, they also pay their own way. 🦗

Alyce Miller

Fiction writer, poet, and essayist Alyce Miller is the author of the novel *Stopping for Green Lights* and a collection of short stories, *The Nature of Longing*, which won the Flannery O'Connor Award for Short Fiction.

Her work has appeared in *The Iowa Review, Fourth Genre, Los Angeles Times* summer fiction issue, *Glimmer Train, Story, Prairie Schooner,* among many others, and her fiction has been awarded the Kenyon Review Award for Literary Excellence in Fiction. A resident of Bloomington, Indiana, Miller is a professor of creative writing at Indiana University and an attorney with a small solo practice.

No Tears for Me, Please

by Jennifer S. Davis

I suffered a mini artistic breakdown several years ago while participating in a Tarantino video night with a friend of mine.

"This is so clever, isn't it?" my friend said, just as John Travolta's character in *Pulp Fiction* accidentally blew out the brains of a kid all over the car window, then proceeded to ponder how to remove the fragments of brain and bone from the backseat.

"Yes," I answered, and promptly began crying, which wasn't a usual state of emotional affairs for me or any of my other now-panicked post–graduate school friends. "I hate clever," I said, and as soon as I said it, it became gospel.

My anti-clever aesthetic quickly seeped over into my analysis of fiction, and I began viewing every emotionally bankrupt, stylistic piece of prose I read as a personal assault. Suddenly, it seemed to me that much of the short fiction heralded as brilliant by the literary powers that be was merely clever, with clever characters who said clever things in clever situations, and just when all of this cleverness got the characters into some type of emotional trouble, the story ended, which left me with the conclusion that perhaps the mere fact that these characters teetered on the precipice of real emotion *was* the story, which I found horrifying and depressing.

So perhaps my anti-clever aesthetic is somewhat in contradiction with what I consider the greatest writing blunder of young writers, although I'd like to think otherwise.

"No tears," I tell my beginning writing students. "No *the tear slid down her cheek, the single tear dazzled in the morning sun, the tear splashed onto the envelope, the tear clung to her lush black feline lashes,*

Genuineness is often sacrificed in order to showcase the author's control over the form and subject matter, the end result technically sound but emotionally empty.

he licked *the river of tears from her freckled cheek, her salty tears mixed with the blue of the sea.* No tears. Period. A character can cry, weep, sob, wail, blubber, lament, but if I see the word *tear* or an approximation thereof …" I let the last of my tirade fade off so that they may conjure their own worst fears of what might happen if they boldly ignore me, which they do consistently.

"How 'bout Shakespeare," one wily student challenged recently. "'How many a holy and obsequious tear / Hath dear religious love stol'n from mine eye.' He's published. And famous."

"True," I said. "But he also wrote in the sixteenth century."

"So?" the student said. "Great art is timeless."

Is it? I have my doubts.

But perhaps the problem I have with highly stylized contemporary films and fiction is that genuineness is often sacrificed in order to showcase the author's or director's control over the form and subject matter, the end result technically sound but emotionally empty, and there is nothing timeless about this effect. This art is a direct product of a society that has been numbed by sophisticated cynicism and so-called wit. So much so, I've noticed in my classes that when a work of fiction tries to be guileless and honest and succeeds by my standards, many of the student readers are often uncomfortable with the display

of emotion. They label the prose as cliché or awkward or gauche, when often it is nothing but fearlessly uncontrived.

And this takes me back to my no-tears rule, which I guess could be seen as a product of our age of cynicism. It's not the symbol of the tear itself that frustrates me, but the tidiness of it. As if all that has gone unsaid in a story, all that we are no longer allowed to write as authors, can be summed up in the ubiquitous image of a tear sliding down a protagonist's cheek. The fact that many beginning writers choose to end their stories this way is telling to me; already they know that certain emotions are too blatant and raw and painful to be written explicitly.

And frankly, well, that makes me sad. 🐛

Jennifer S. Davis

Jennifer S. Davis won the Iowa Short Fiction Award for *Her Kind of Want*. She is the recipient of the Prague Summer Seminars Fellowship in Fiction, a Djerassi Residency, and a Washington Artist Trust Fellowship. Her stories have been published in such journals as *The Paris Review*, *Oxford American*, *One Story*, and *The Georgia Review*. Originally from Alabama, Jennifer has taught at the University of Miami and Eastern Washington University.

Circling the Unsayable

by Jocelyn Lieu

Writing first drafts of stories means whipping out words to trap my daydreams. I don't think about language; instead, I try to describe the daydreams and what the people in them are doing.

When I read the above paragraph, it feels neat and untrue. It implies I perceive the dreams that become my fiction as clearly as I do the world outside my skin. That's a lie, of course. Though the dreams at the core of my stories start from everyday life, they soon become imagination's mist and shadows. The shadows move, change. Writing nails them in time, where I can see and study them, and color them back to life.

Here I can't help thinking of Jackson Pollock, who poured, spattered, and lashed the canvas with strings of paint. His process was about snaring not only a vision but the moment the vision occurred to him. The paint becomes a net cast around something too fast to be caught. The bare spaces between the net's strands are as significant as the strands themselves because they hint at what can't be painted, can't be described.

Writing first drafts is flinging nets of words around dreamed moments that defy capture.

So I fly. I hurl words and don't pay them mind (unless I'm hearing my characters' voices and trying to record them). Writing first drafts isn't a quiet business. I mutter, jiggle my legs, get up to dance, preferably to Mozart or Neil Young and Crazy Horse.

After I hit the "Save" key, I look at what I've written. Pollock, done laying down paint, would isolate sections of canvas with a stretching frame, trying to find the painting within the painting. First I find the story. Then, within that frame, I delete untrue words that don't glow with magic. Unnecessary words also get sent into cyber-nothingness, as do garish ones that detract from the story. Words that survive help me re-enter the story-dream—not the dream that started it all, because it's already shape-changed out of existence, but the dream as it grows, gains specificity, and takes on the illusion of life.

If I've written well, I've dived into the unconscious the way the surrealists did and returned with some of the unconscious's veined ore. When I revise, I go back to the lode and scratch more deeply, deliberately in. Though revision

I strive for transparency; I want readers to feel they're not stuck on the page but can see through my sentences directly to the story.

is less Dionysian than writing first drafts, it's possibly more pleasurable (though it can be torture, too): a conscious shaping that locates story-dreams in a vivid medium where they may last and even generate faint rays of original power.

The surrealists, generally speaking, were more interested in process than the end result. Not me. I'm an obsessive rewriter. I craft the hell out my work and can complete twenty or more drafts (by which I mean printed-out drafts, not computer diddling) of a single story. My goal is to make language as simple and true as possible. I strive for transparency; I want readers to feel they're not stuck on the page but can see through my sentences directly to the story. I want them to feel the story's life.

In this spirit I have a rule, which I break again and again: to use words modestly. Words should masquerade as ordinary. Thus, for example, I don't shy away from *to be* and *she said*. I try to say things as simply as I can, not because I'm a particularly demure writer but because doing so acknowledges words' seismic power.

Simplicity means—to the extent it's possible, since language, like plutonium, is enriched by past usage—that I'm not lazily riding on another writer's back. I am not saying make it new every time, an impossibility; but when I allude, I do so sparingly. Even though I'm schooled by all the good (and bad) books I've ever read, I steer away from open acknowledgement of this fact in my fiction. Allusions, after all, declare first allegiance to literature instead of the sensations of lived life.

If your work as a writer is to circle the unsayable, language both helps and crushes you. Words are the means, but they also have their own agenda. They rebel, take over, and often I let them, enjoying the rebellion. Revision becomes a sweet struggle. Whenever I use obviously figurative language, or wield words that otherwise call attention to themselves (like *wield*), I'm going against my aesthetics. I'm also quietly howling with delight, because working with language, calling on words' old power to move, is such fucking fun. ❦

Joceyln Lieu

Jocelyn Lieu, who lives in New York City, is the author of a collection of stories, *Potential Weapons*. She is a graduate of the Warren Wilson College and teaches writing at Parsons School of Design.

Four Rules

by Jane Yolen

I *hate* writing rules. I *hate* imposing them on others. Mine work for me. If they work for you, fine. If not, feel free to ignore them. They are very simple.

1. Eschew the exclamation point! If your prose is not exciting all on its own, a screamer (as it has been called in some circles, though not mine) is hardly going to help.

2. Go relatively easy on adverbs. There is a rumor that a stand-alone volume could have been made just using all the adverbs in J.K. Rowling's fourth Harry Potter book. But I can't say that for sure, as I bombed out on my Harry Potter reading after the third book and use the tomes now only to keep various doors open.

3. Don't let your characters float on the page. Unless, of course, they are birds, fairies, superheroes, or jet pilots. By that I mean

anchor them with some action. Don't let them just talk and talk and talk. In theater, actors always have some bit of "business" that keeps their characters rooted in the real world. Even the birds, fairies, superheroes, or jet pilots.

4. Have fun writing. If it's all agony, take up some other line of work. I know I would. I'm not a masochist, after all, and I don't play one in the movies either. 🍎

Jane Yolen

Jane Yolen has been called America's Hans Christian Andersen and a modern-day Aesop; her many books and stories have won several awards, including the Caldecott Medal, the Nebula Award, and the Jewish Book Award.

The Semicolon and the Infrequency of Its Use

by Vincent Standley

A mere mark to which no sound or power is ever given, cannot be a letter; though it may, like the marks used for punctuation, deserve a name and a place in grammar. Commas, semicolons, and the like, represent silence, rather than sounds, and are therefore not letters.

—*The Grammar of English Grammars* (1862)

Very early in the sixteenth century, the Italian printer Aldus Manutius began using the semicolon to join interdependent statements. A century later it had been incorporated into English punctuation. Shakespeare and John Donne—or their typesetters—used it, while English grammarians argued for its use as an elocutionary mark to indicate pauses (comma, 1; semicolon, 2; colon, 3). Ben Jonson, though, was the first to systematize its use as a syntactical mark. In *English Grammar*, he writes, "A Semicolon is a distinction of an imperfect Sentence, wherein with somewhat a longer Breath, the Sentence following is included." Popular use reached its height during the eighteenth century. By 1900, use of the semicolon had diminished to the level we know today. And barring a bit more variation—in Victorian novels semicolons and colons are sometimes interchangeable, and in letters a semicolon may follow an abbreviated title or salutation—its function has remained fairly constant on both sides of the Atlantic. In England, *The Grammar of English Grammars* states:

The Semicolon is used to separate those parts of a compound sentence, which are neither so closely connected as those which are distinguished by the comma, nor so little dependent as those which require the colon.

And in America, *Murray's English Grammar* (1821) explains:

> The semicolon is sometimes used when the preceding member of the sentence does not itself give a complete sense, but depends on the following clause ... and sometimes when the sense of that member would be complete without the concluding one.

In today's usage, the semicolon may function to contrast two statements in the same manner as a comma + conjunction, or it

A recent statistical analysis of punctuation use from the sixteenth through the twentieth centuries concludes that, based on how often it is used, the semicolon is so minor a punctuation mark that giving it equal space alongside other marks is entirely unjustified.

may be followed by a conjunctive adverb. The semicolon can also be used to create a hierarchy of order when a complex series would otherwise be confusing.

Colons, dashes, and semicolons are all intermediate marks. They come between clauses. But the semicolon has the further distinction of being in-between punctuation marks: It is neither a period nor a comma. Rather, it is a hybrid that can replace or be replaced by its two parts. Or, as the *Encyclopædia Britannica* puts it, the semicolon is halfway between the comma and the period. The usefulness of most punctuation is rooted in its necessity and the stability of its function. I know when to use a comma, and I know the effect it will have on a sentence. Moreover, I can distinguish the need for a comma from the need for a period. And where a colon functions more like a semantic *equals* sign, the semicolon indicates a less specific relationship. Without the semicolon some clarity or nuance might be lost, but no sentence absolutely needs one. There are always other marks or arrangements that will do.

Practical discussions of the semicolon tend to be cautionary. In college writing handbooks, it and the colon are often bridled with the warning *Do not overuse*. Similarly, no one is surprised when a writer writing on writing says use of the semicolon should be restricted, and under no circumstance should it be used in dialog. These positions are perfectly reasonable. The semicolon can be intrusive, even jarring, and though it may be used intentionally for this effect, convention usually dictates a more transparent use of punctuation.

A recent statistical analysis of punctuation use from the sixteenth through the twentieth centuries concludes that, based on how often it is used, the semicolon is so minor a punctuation mark that giving it equal space alongside other marks is entirely unjustified. The conclusion is bolstered by the estimate that commas and periods account for 90 percent of the punctuation used in English. If value and necessity were judged by quantity of use, the other 10 percent would be irrelevant punctuation marks, or worse: anachronisms, museum curiosities, junk.

The Oxford Companion to the English Language presents a more psychological explanation as to the unpopularity of the semicolon: "The semicolon is often avoided in ordinary writing, or replaced with a dash, because many users lack confidence in it." This statement suggests a kind of low-level anxiety. What other punctuation mark could be said to inspire a lack of confidence? Part of the trouble may lie in the semicolon's condition of being both and neither. How do you know when to use something that functions as a period *and* a comma, as not a period *and* not a comma? And once you know, how do you characterize the effect it has on a sentence? In particular, when it functions in place of a comma + conjunction, the effect becomes particularly hard to isolate. This may be more a consequence of what it does not do than what it does do. The pairing of two statements with a comma + conjunction implies a more immediate relationship than the same statements separated by a period. We assume the statements are interdependent. But the conjunction also informs the nature of the interdependence and provides an angle of approach: *and, but, or, yet, nor, for, so.* The semicolon elides the angle of approach. It frames the interdependence but does not tell us how to proceed. The refusal to tell is a productive way to present what cannot be told. At the same time, not telling can strengthen what has *already* been told. The semicolon is a useful tool for enacting these effects. Elision, though, easily becomes gratuitous, and the utility of the semicolon may be sustained by the infrequency of its use. ❦

Vincent Standley

Vincent Standley is the editor of *3rd Bed*.

42

On Advice
by S.L. Wisenberg

1. When I was an undergrad, back during the Carter administration, I took an expository writing class with a fairly famous essayist and editor. He was so famous and formal (he was a short Jewish Chicagoan and he wished to be Max Beerbohm, the Gentile British critic and cartoonist; I don't know Beerbohm's physical stature, but he was knighted). In class I was always Miss Wisenberg, and I was so afraid of the teacher, so afraid, in fact, that I couldn't bring myself to read his comments on my papers, which we never had to revise. Only later, much later, when I mustered up the courage to read them (when the class was long over and I no longer had to be afeared) did I find that he had written, on every single essay, next to my every contraction (each of which he had circled), "a contraction worth avoiding," over and over in his neat hand.

Rule of thumb: Always read the comments that your teachers, friends, and peers bother to write on your work. You don't have to agree with what they write or follow their advice, but you should seek to understand their suggestions and objections and ask them if you have questions. By the way, I think that just about every contraction is worth using, depending on the formality of your work. In other words, I think Joseph Epstein was wrong.

2. The first story I wrote in grad school (first Reagan administration) came out of our first class discussion on ethnicity, back before the topic was so mandatory as to be boring. When my turn came to tell "what you are," there was a gasp in the workshop: a Jew from Texas! Such a specimen had never been heard of, apparently, in Iowa City. I went home and wrote a two-part autobiographical story from

I think that just about every contraction is worth using, depending on the formality of your work. In other words, I think Joseph Epstein was wrong.

the point of view of a young teenager in Houston. My teacher told me that it should be three parts and that I should write a novel. I didn't. Seven years later I rewrote the piece in a distant, ironic third person, broken into many parts, without looking at the original. It has been published in three anthologies and won me an Illinois Arts Council fellowship and became the title story of my collection (reign of Bush the Younger).

Rule of thumb: Sometimes advice may be good, but you can't follow it. I didn't know how to make the story have three parts, I didn't know how to make it into a novel. I had to let the piece settle and wait for the re-vision.

3. In Miami (Reagan administration) I started a writing group. I presented a story I'd written the last semester of the workshop. One member, a Yale philosophy major who covered baseball for the *Miami Herald*, suggested I make the second half the first half. I did.

Rule of thumb: Sometimes advice is easy and good. The story was published a couple of years later in *Another Chicago Magazine* (Reagan), won an Illinois Literary Award, and was published later (Clinton) in an anthology.

4. I started writing a novel (Bush the Elder). I spent two months in Europe doing research. I extracted some parts of the manuscript-in-progress to use in essays. I filled a file drawer with bits of the novel. Two excerpts were published (Bush the Younger). Many years, many presidents, many wars after I started, I wrote and rewrote, rethought, revised, agonized. I got married. My friend S. said, "I need to know who the main character lives with, what are the details of her life." P. said, "You're having so much trouble

with it because you're really a nonfiction writer." (My nonfiction book was published in 2002.) In fall 2004 (Bush the Younger) I decided—eureka!—how to arrange and conceive of the book. The next February I decided again. I wrung my hands. I kept thinking of a story I read as a child: There once was a girl named Rosa who worked as a seamstress, but she wanted to paint. One day she broke her needle. That was it. She threw down her sewing. The next day, she went to the studio with her artist father. Her name was (drum roll) Rosa Bonheur, famous nineteenth-century painter and sculptor, her work in museums everywhere.

Rule of thumb: You will wonder: Is the work hard because you're following the wrong path? Or because it's just hard? Are you breaking your needle or your paintbrush?

You may never know. 🐛

S.L. Wisenberg

S.L. Wisenberg is the author of *Holocaust Girls: History, Memory & Other Obsessions* and *The Sweetheart Is In.* She dispenses advice at Northwestern and Roosevelt universities and is the creative nonfiction editor of *Another Chicago Magazine.* She has published work in several genres in *The New Yorker, Nerve, Ploughshares,* and *Tikkun.*

Sleep On It

by Heid E. Erdrich

Write before you wake. Write as you sleep, if at all possible. Download a draft into your dreams—it can be done. It will be done. In fact, try to keep your mind from copying work off.

Your brain scans and spies like software running somewhere in the background. Your wetware knows what you've been writing and it won't forget revisions and versions and words that got away. So let it go when day ends and you let go your cares. Let your unconscious mind have a go at your latest draft as you drift off. She's a keen editor, an intuitive, ready to take leaps, so like yourself you'll think you've met your match. Tell her you trust her. Imagine you hand her your work in a great big stack. Tell her, "Take a stab and get back to me in the morning."

Sleep solves all problems, plays creative to our critic, lets another eye see what in draft surpasses understanding, reveals meaning and vivid images that tie ideas together with loops of animated twine strung between paragraphs or lines—or in red-pen margin notes that speak in squeaky voices and loom large just before daylight hits the room.

Our unconscious self, with uncanny knack, can hold whole pages in files we'd never find awake. Something asleep, some sub-program organizes every insight, deletes what we do not need. Better, that sleeping self can see its way where words get us lost and work loose threads into metaphor's nets.

Best at allusions, illustrations and conclusions, the dreaming drafter knows what it is we were after, knows how we can get from A to B to C. And it has vast stretches of time to work out what tires us in an hour. It powers through to conclude. It never gets carpal tunnel, never stops for coffee, a walk, to talk, for chocolate. It never even stops to sleep.

Sleep your way to the stop. Full stop. End stop. ❧

Heid E. Erdrich
Heid Erdrich has published three books and teaches at the University of St. Thomas in St. Paul, Minnesota.

Enough Already

by Steven Barthelme

I tried to think of a personal rule I use in making stories and came up with nothing, such things usually being so much second nature as to be, if not unconscious, at least forgotten. It's the same problem that sometimes occurs in teaching undergraduates when you throttle some poor child for switching point of view in the middle of a sentence, say, and then have to remember—because you have to *say*—why not. Or worse, on those slow days, when you start wondering if any of the things you teach could be shown to be present in your own work and, of course, can't think of any. Then I tried to think whether I *ever* had had a rule, and then recalled one, though one which had nothing to do with images or significant detail or Aristotelian dramatic structure. It was: No more cats.

It wasn't always so. When I started out, cats were in every story and in most of the nonfiction pieces as well, in spite of that other rule that says when the conversation turns to cats, it's time for the host to start cleaning up and the guests to go home. Still, you write about things you're passionate about, if you have any sense at all, and cats were such for me—one in particular of course, a gray fellow who was one of my tutors way back when.

For example, I wrote of a separating couple quarrelling over who gets the cat, stealing it back and forth; and in another piece a picture of the sleepy cat on the bedspread watching the telephone beside him ring—it's the boyfriend, long distance for the girlfriend, imagining the cat, longing for its serenity. There's a story about a talking cat, of course, another made of wood, one with a limp wrist and gold eyes who begs like a dog, and one that walks upright—everybody calls him Tutu. By the time I published a collection, the few reviewers all mentioned this predilection, perhaps alerted by John Barth, another of my tutors, who had kindly consented to write a jacket blurb, in which he noted the crowd of cats inside.

At which point I swore off fictional cats. Could've switched to dogs, which I also like, but that seemed like cheating, like writing those stories which are certainly not about a writer (as the catechism requires them not to be), but instead feature a beguiling but troubled painter, jeweler, architect, musician, ad man, or ne'er-do-well who in his or her off hours talks very fancy and broods about László Moholy-Nagy and such. More cleverly, it's an intellectually tilted plumber. Dogs were a dodge.

So I had a rule: No stories in which a cat played any significant part (cousin of another rule, enforced on students, concerning Elvis). And I did it, succeeded. I wrote at least a half-dozen pieces, maybe eight, maybe ten. A prominent snake, a coachwhip, figured in one, and a number of others concerned children, which I think of as sort of cat surrogates, but not a real cat in sight.

And these stories weren't all that bad, by which I mean they weren't any worse than the feline-equipped stories that preceded them. If there was a hole in the story, a yawning—strike that—a gaping space where the cat was absent, I didn't notice, couldn't tell. In the whole (unpublished) second collection, there were probably no more than two or six cats. I was cured.

One needs an obsession, damned hard to write without one. I wrote about cars and lawns.

Still, one needs an obsession, damned hard to write without one. I wrote about cars and lawns. There were a number of pieces featuring old people. I've always been sort of interested in the Catholic Church, in which I was raised in the last of its real hoodoo days; I could use that. But I wouldn't say it's an obsession, exactly.

And, anyway, if artists can paint the same painting over and over, Ad Reinhardt with all his black squares and such, or Monet producing haystack after haystack, and if Fitzgerald can write his rich girls again and again, if Chekhov's Vanyas and Jean Rhys's Mr. Mackenzies can reappear with their names changed in play after play and novel after novel ... what's the big deal? Gee, James, can't you write about something besides focking Ireland!? Sure, I'm not them, I know; it's not the same thing, I know. Cats, Jesus. So I've got third-rate obsessions. What can I say? It's God's will.

My new rule is that lines in a rag-right typescript must come out roughly the same, within two or three or four characters of each other; this, I find, returns writing to what it always should be, a form of play—although it also sometimes requires the insertion of useless words (which is how *or four* got into this sentence), or the deletion of *le mot juste*. C'est la vie.

Rules are essential. Make yourself some, all you want, strong, logical, bracing, inviolable, iron rules. Feel shame when you break them, and delicious moral superiority when you don't. Nothing is more entertaining. After I wrote the ten catless stories, a predictable thing happened. Cats snuck in. Sidled in. In the latest story, nineteen of them. And I've started work on a novel. Stars a veterinarian. ❦

Steven Barthelme

A professor of English at the University of Southern Mississippi, Steven Barthelme publishes widely in literary magazines. He has published a story collection, *And He Tells the Little Horse the Whole Story*, and won a Pushcart Prize in 1993. His nonfiction has appeared in *The New York Times Magazine*, *Los Angeles Times*, *The Washington Post*, and elsewhere, and his fiction has been published in, among many others, *McSweeney's*, *The Yale Review*, and *The Atlantic Monthly*.

With a Frond Like Me Who Needs Anemone

by Molly Giles

I would love to share my private writing tips, tricks, tics, and tools of the trade, but the sad truth is, I have none. I write when I can about whatever it is I am thinking about at the time. I am dull. I do, however, have many interesting friends, most of whom write successfully and several of whom are actually famous. Here, in alphabetical order, are the secrets they entrusted me with.

A writes in earphones listening to Kitaro: the same tape, over and over. **B**, who grew up in Calcutta, blasts a different television show from every room of her big Berkeley house. **C** uses the word *suddenly* to jumpstart him into the next scene. **D** worries worry beads. **E** imagines someone is standing with a gun at his head. **F** takes the baby out of the playpen and crawls in herself with a bottle. **G** has a different Bible chapter come up on his computer screen every morning. **H** types *The End* before he begins. **I** starts a new book on a certain day each January; if she finishes it before the year is up, she does not write again for the rest of the year. **J** writes with her three dogs on her couch in front of the weather channel. **K** can only write by the ocean, at night, in longhand. **L** can only write during the summer, in daylight, in Microsoft Word.

> *I am dull. I do, however, have many interesting friends ... Here, in alphabetical order, are the secrets they entrusted me with.*

M wears a blindfold and types in thirty-minute segments to a kitchen timer. N gets inspiration in the car wash. O loses his advance at the race track and writes to get out of debt. P uses mauve legal pads. Q refinished the floors of his house and it wasn't even his house, it was a rental. R keeps a mirror on her desk, puts on a different hat for every character in her book, and talks in voices. S takes her laptop to Starbucks, where she joins her friend T and the two write until it is time to pick their children up from day care. U reads the tarot; if the Tower comes up reversed, she goes back to bed. V hates his name but won't change it because W told him it was bad luck to change once you got published and T has been published and W has not, although W, who takes deadlines seriously, did at least finish his novel when the doctor said he had cancer (he's in remission). X sees a woman's bent shape in the knotty pine paneling of his trailer and prays, *Please please help me*. Y has a photo tacked above his computer of James Joyce with his legs apart, hands in pockets, and hat tipped back; he pretends Joyce is peeing words onto the screen. Z finds inspiration in sleep and when A takes her earphones off he puts them on and wakes up at midnight full of dumb ideas.

I hope these tips help other writers. They have not helped me. The only thing that has ever helped me is learning early that the answer to *Can you keep a secret?* is yes. ❧

Molly Giles

Molly Giles is the author of two short story collections, *Rough Translations* and *Creek Walk*, and a novel, *Iron Shoes*. She has won a National Book Critics Circle Award for book reviewing, a National Endowment for the Arts award, the 2003 O. Henry Prize, and two Pushcart Prizes. She currently directs the creative writing program at the University of Arkansas in Fayetteville.

Make It More Complex

by Peter Turchi

I remind myself to make a story more complex when it seems one-dimensional, single-minded, predictable, familiar, or thoroughly understandable. Often the first draft of a story will feel flat, its options limited; I've allowed the events, dialogue, and characters' lives to become too narrowly focused. *Make it more complex* is my reminder to cultivate another aspect of the main character's life, a secondary character, a secondary line of investigation, a tertiary line of investigation, a pattern of images—something intriguing that is not (yet, apparently) directly related to whatever has become the story's whirlpool, its enormous, powerful, potentially reductive vortex.

Some writers need to have the ending of a story—or *an* ending—in mind before they can begin. Others of us have trouble writing a story if we (think we) know the ending. The problem with

knowing where you're going is a problem of over-determination—of limiting a story's possibilities from the outset, so that the writing is an execution of a notion, a literary equivalent of a mathematical proof. If I suspect I know a story's ending before I've started writing, I need either to write past that ending (*So then what?*) or to consider which of the givens along the way bear further exploration—ways to add to the story's journey, and to make it more complex.

For writers of conventional realism, the ongoing challenge is to create characters of realistic psychological complexity. This means constantly working to allow characters to think more, and differently; to allow them to be self-conscious, self-critical, and contradictory. There's an element of perversity to this, because writing about simple-minded people facing clearly delineated conflicts is easier. So another way to state the rule would be: *Make it more difficult. Increase your ambition.* For writers of fiction other than psychological realism, the challenge might be to avoid writing to a thesis, or to avoid creating work that merely illustrates a design strategy. *What more can this be? What more should this be?* These are questions we ask ourselves in order to *make it more complex.*

Do I need to acknowledge that there is beauty in the austere, that we admire Shaker furniture, primitive paintings, and the song of a single voice? Complexity in itself is no virtue.

> *Others of us have trouble writing a story if we (think we) know the ending. The problem with knowing where you're going is a problem of over-determination.*

Rules are reductive, rules are constraining, rules are what the beginner wants and the experienced distrust. Create rules, follow them; but know when to ignore them. Like any rule that comes to mind—to my mind, anyway—this one immediately leads me to recognize the virtue of its opposite. But that in itself is a demonstration of the need to *make it more complex: Question every rule.* 🐛

Peter Turchi

Peter Turchi, whose most recent book is *Maps of the Imagination: The Writer as Cartographer*, is director of the Warren Wilson MFA Program for Writers. He is co-editor, with Andrea Barrett, of *The Story Behind the Story: 26 Stories by Contemporary Writers and How They Work* and, with Charles Baxter, of *Bringing the Devil to His Knees: The Craft of Fiction and the Writing Life.*

56

We Are Not Your Mother

by Janice Eidus

Never, never assume that, because your main character is a thinly disguised version of *you*, and because you and your mother think that you're terrific, your readers will feel the same way. We are not *you*; we are not your mother. We do not offer you, or your literary alter ego, unconditional love. On the page, you need to *earn*, if not our total, all-consuming, head-over-heels, gaga love, at least our interest and sympathy (and perhaps even our respect).

Here's an example of what I'm talking about: A couple of years ago, a friend was working on a novel. There are a number of things I like and admire about her. She's intelligent, well-read, witty, generous, and loyal to her friends. There are also a number of things that I don't especially like and admire about her. For instance, she's so spoiled that, at thirty-five, she still expects her wealthy parents to support her financially while she flits from career to career. At the same time, she whines and whines about being single, and then proceeds to dump one man after another because none are "perfect." In other words, I like her, but not unconditionally.

Still, when she asked me to critique her novel-in-progress, I agreed. It turned out to be very autobiographical, about a single, thirty-five-year-old woman who buys a fabulous New York City penthouse with her parents' money and hops (not surprisingly) from career to career and man to man. All the while, she complains about how tough her life is. *Shut up!* I found myself thinking over and over as I turned the pages.

After I'd read the novel, my friend and I met for coffee. "What did you think?" she asked eagerly.

You need to earn, if not our total, all-consuming, head-over-heels, gaga love, at least our interest and sympathy.

I took a deep breath. "I didn't really like Samantha. I didn't want to hang out with her for 450 pages."

Across the table, my friend appeared to grow angry, her cheeks inflamed. "You're saying," she cried, "that you don't like me!"

"No, I do like you." I tried to remain calm. "You're funny, smart, loyal, and generous. But," I sighed, "Samantha isn't any of those things. She's just spoiled and *kvetchy*, with no self awareness, no irony, no objectivity, no vulnerability."

My friend lit a cigarette. "Go on," she said, tight-lipped. "I'm listening."

"Maybe," I said, "Samantha could occasionally acknowledge to herself that she has some issues, and that she herself isn't perfect." I paused to sip my black tea. "And maybe she could acknowledge that her pampered lifestyle is hardly the stuff of Dickens." As mildly as I could, I added, "She's not *entitled* to my interest, you know."

The waiter came over, and my friend and I paid the check. Outside the café, her goodbye hug was perfunctory. I walked away, deciding to give her time to cool off and to process what I'd said. Six months later, she called to ask if I would be willing to read her revised novel.

Partly out of curiosity and partly out of friendship, I agreed. A week later, I sat down with her novel and quickly discovered, to my surprise and profound relief, that Samantha now possessed both humor and self-awareness about her neuroses and imperfections. She'd become a far more interesting and nuanced character, someone quite nice to spend time with.

My friend's novel is just one example. As a teacher of writing, a book reviewer, and a reader, I'm constantly coming across work in which the protagonist—clearly the author's alter ego/stand-in—feels automatically entitled not only to my total sympathy, but also to my full engagement and unquestioning admiration.

Here's another example: An African American writer I know loathes the very concept of affirmative action. In the novel he's working on, the hero constantly espouses *his* antipathy toward affirmative action as well as toward those characters (his nemeses) that support affirmative action. These opposing characters are each presented as one-dimensional idiots and buffoons. Clearly, the author presumes that readers will automatically agree and sympathize with his hero's viewpoint. But I—and many of his potential readers—support affirmative action. So, while reading the novel, I found myself irritated not only by the hero for his rigid, unnuanced views, but also by the author for his unbalanced, one-dimensional portraits of the characters who share *my* views.

Now, this isn't at all to say that I need to agree with the political and philosophical opinions of literary characters, or endorse their actions, in order to find them sympathetic. The truth is that I adore Raskolnikov, that murderous fellow—and he's not the only literary rascal I've adored in my lifetime, not by a long shot. If, for instance, the affirmative action–hating character (who, of course, is a far cry from being a murderer) had offered some thoughtful reasons for his views, if he had done some soul-searching, if he had possessed a tad of humility, my sympathies might have been engaged. Even a supremely arrogant character, rendered three-dimensional and complex, can be extremely interesting.

So, to sum up: Dear Writer, we readers were not present at your birth (nor at the birth of your fictional alter ego). We haven't nursed you through measles and chicken pox, haven't applauded your first baby steps. We don't love you like a mother, and we never will. However, if you work really, really hard at seducing and engaging us on the page, we might just fall a little bit in love with you and your character(s)—at least for the duration of your novel. 🐛

Janice Eidus

Novelist, short story writer, and essayist Janice Eidus has twice won the O. Henry Prize for her short stories, as well as a Redbook Prize and Pushcart Prize.

Her new novel, *The War of the Rosens*, is about an eccentric Bronx Jewish family. She writes frequently about issues of Jewish identity (sometimes with humor, and always with affection). She holds a MA in fiction from Johns Hopkins.

The Five Senses

by Stewart O'Nan

One rule of thumb (which includes the thumb, you'll see) I try to keep in mind while I'm actually sitting at my machine is the rule of the five senses. I like fiction that brings the reader physically or sensually into an imaginary world by use of concrete detail. I'm a visual person (have twenty-ten vision, will never have to wear glasses, can read the airline's name off the tail of the 757 passing overhead), so I tend to include too much visual detail and not enough olfactory, tactile, etc. So when I'm sitting there working, to remind myself, I'll take my hand and spread

I learned how I could suggest sensory detail rather than state it plain, saving even more time and space and letting the reader do more work and become a co-author.

my five fingers out sea-urchin-spine straight and then set the vein side of my wrist on top of my head and wear those fingers like a mohawk.

I don't know exactly when I started this—probably early on, when I was just learning to set scenes. The result was that my first efforts were choked with background detail (why use two details when I could imagine five?), but the prompt did make me delve further into whatever imaginary world I was trying to keep the reader in. Later, a friend said that I was including things merely because I *could* see or feel or hear them, not because the reader (or character) needed to, and that was a great help.

Later still (this is still early on), I learned how I could suggest sensory detail rather than state it plain, saving even more time and space and letting the reader do more work and become a co-author. That 757 we saw before comes with its own whining turbines, and a good reader may even toss in a decaying contrail behind it, a hint of wind in the upper atmosphere, sun glinting off the tail's aluminum skin. But first I have to imagine it and leave the correct space. If my characters are standing ankle deep in a warm pond in the middle of the woods and suddenly look up, then, yes, that plane's going to make noise without me having to foley it in.

The movies do everything with sight and sound, and blatantly. Using impingement to convey the five senses shows the true power of words—their flexibility and suggestibility—which, for me, is why (though I love movies) reading will always be a richer, more exciting experience. There's simply more there, and I get to help.

So while writing, ask yourself, *When's the last time I included a smell, or a texture, or a taste?* And, on a much higher level, *Is this detail essential—that is, does it somehow reflect the path of my character's desires?* And, when called for, *Can I do it more powerfully—really make it stick—by letting the reader discover it him- or herself?* And if you can't remember all this, just put your hand on top of your head like a rooster's comb and it will all come back to you. First, though, close the door. ❦

Stewart O'Nan

Stewart O'Nan's award-winning fiction includes *Snow Angels*, *The Names of the Dead*, *The Speed Queen*, *A World Away*, *A Prayer for the Dying*, *Everyday People*, and the story collection *In the Walled City*. In 1996, *Granta* named him one of America's best young novelists.

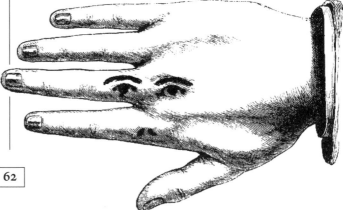

The Very Rule

by Jill Christman

Somewhere along the way—maybe as far back as middle school language arts, but definitely in my undergrad fiction class, and then driven home by everyone from Strunk and White to the helpful obsessive in my first grad-school workshop who returned every manuscript with a tally of deadweight words—I learned that *very* was bad. *Very* is one of the forbidden words my brain stores alongside prose-littering qualifiers, the sentence-slowing *suddenly*, and, of course, every indolent adverb that hangs on the arm of a perfectly competent verb like a bad boyfriend you know you're better off without.

We might spew out *very* in our everyday speech, but writing isn't talking. In every creative writing class, eventually I'll hear myself say something like this: Very *is like a red flag waving in your prose. Hello?*

Hello? This writer didn't work hard enough here. This writer knows she hasn't chosen the right word.

I say things like this because somewhere around the middle of the term when I've been wrestling with image and meaning and wordplay and all of the elusive things that make writing *writing*, I get desperate: I want to stand up at the front of the class and say something that makes sense. I want to teach something teachable, and I want my students to hear it and learn it. I want something in the muck and mire of the writing class to be simple. *These, folks, are the rules.* Very *is a very bad word.*

My pedant self talks sense, but here is my confession: I am prone to hyperbole. I can't help myself. I have a dramatic streak. I am drawn to all things *very*. My sentences long to stretch themselves thin with

The word I'm avoiding when I avoid very is the one that means "extremely"—that much-loathed adverbial form. That's the one I know I can't use. But I do.

very, but I pull them back, stout them up, reach up with the padding ring finger of my right hand, tat, tat, tat, tat on Backspace, and bring the curtain down on *very*'s theatrics.

Now that I'm thinking about *very*, I hear it everywhere, especially coming out of my own mouth. But, then again, I am mother to a toddler, and toddlers are creatures of excess, no? Even if she can't yet say it, my daughter loves the sense of the word, the way it pushes the next word to its limits—*very* big, *very* fun, *very* far. Because of this, writers of children's books don't have to play by our sensible rules. Eric Carle's famously greedy caterpillar is *very* hungry, the spider *very* busy, the firefly *very* lonely, and the cricket *very* quiet. Shhhhh. Note these creatures aren't ravenous, frantic, isolated, or mute—no. They are what Carle tells us they are, but more so and better.

But me? I'm supposed to write for grown-ups. And good, grown-up writers don't indulge themselves with *very*. Or, at least, we try to resist.

I decided to do an empirical study on the use of very in my memoir *Darkroom: A Family Exposure*. Here are the results.

Total words: 86, 418

Total uses of *very*: 42

Percentage of *very*s in all of *Darkroom*: .048

Now, before we start wagging fingers, let's break this down. Twenty-four of these *very*s appear in quotations, so I can't be blamed for that, right? For example, my dad reports he was not a "very good father," my mom defends my father by claiming that *his* mother was "very controlling," and the prison chaplain is "very sorry" to tell me that my uncle bled to death in his cell. Indeed. I suppose here I should confess that one of the twenty-four quoted *very*s emerges from the invisible lips of a therapist character I manufactured for the purposes of the book. *Wait, you say, you said this was memoir—you can't manufacture a character in memoir!* Oh dear.

Eighteen *very*s remain for me to call my own (or .02 percent of the total words)—a statistically insignificant number, but for a writer who claims she doesn't let herself use *very*,

perhaps not. Again, the situation is more complicated than the numbers imply. The earliest, unquoted use of *very* appears midway through chapter five— "the very first ovulation"—soon followed by another use: "the very thought that this was my first funeral." I think we can cut me some slack here. What we

have in chapter five is two firsts: the fear of a pubescent pregnancy and a dead grandmother. Not only that, both *very*s are of the kinder, gentler adjectival variety, the former emphasizing "the full sense of the term," and the latter, something like "actual"—as in, the *very* place, the *very* book, the *very* dog who bit me on the leg in the park. This *very* allows us to pinpoint a specific something, and isn't particularity the name of the writing game?

The word I'm avoiding when I avoid *very* is the one that means "extremely"—that much-loathed adverbial form. That's the one I know I can't use. But I do. In *Darkroom*, I used *very* as an adverb six times: "very small," "very good," "very carefully," "very bad." In two of these six instances, having somehow breached security in my editor brain, I go word-wild and double up, claiming that on the occasion of my first visit to a therapist " ... I was tired—very, very tired" and dismissing my miscreant lover's excuse for his blatant infidelity: "I didn't believe him. Not very often, I thought. It's not very often that people change all that much."

There we'd sat, on a steamy porch in Alabama, and with his eyes flicking from the lip of his beer bottle to the ants on the railing and back again, this guy told me with a straight face that sometimes love just changes, people change—and I had the good sense to call him a liar. You know, suddenly, thinking about that treacherous creep sneaking off into the stockroom with his saucy sous-chef, I feel just a bit less guilty for letting *very* slip into my prose—I mean, in writing, as in life, you can end up with a bad boyfriend who behaves abysmally, talks incessantly, and cheats like a low-down dirty dog, right? For these guys, we must reserve some very bad words. 🐜

Jill Christman

Jill Christman's memoir *Darkroom: A Family Exposure* won the AWP Award for Creative Nonfiction. She holds an MFA from the University of Alabama and teaches writing at Ball State University.

Write When You Feel Lousy

by Dinty W. Moore

Write when you feel lousy: The rule seems counterintuitive. If you give it a test run, your inner voices will scream, "No, no, not right now, this is a horrible idea, please stop!" The experience almost always begins poorly. On certain days, only a committed masochist can really make it work. But this rule of thumb is worth all of that.

Write when you feel lousy is more than just another variation on the old adage *keep your butt in the seat*, though that's a good one too.

My experience, hard-earned and sometimes excruciating, goes like this:

1. Writing on days when I'd rather curl up into a ball under the cotton comforter eventually takes my mind off of feeling so lousy.

2. Pain does something interesting to the brain.

The first effect is valuable in and of itself, and likely due to the simple powers of distraction. The second effect, the interesting one, is almost certainly endorphins.

Endorphins are why long-distance runners experience runner's high. The harder you exercise, the more endorphins your body makes, and elevated endorphin levels lead to feelings of euphoria.

Endorphins are also natural painkillers.

So when I'm in pain—let's say I wake up one morning and my sinus cavities are open wounds, swollen, and drenched in battery acid—my body instinctively pumps endorphins into the brain. I don't feel euphoric, because this is not the same as exercise, and my head still hurts, but the endorphins do what they do.

Pain does something interesting to the brain.

I don't claim to fully understand the neuroscience, but I understand this: If I tough it out—keep to my writing schedule, glue my fingers firmly to the keyboard, lean into whatever it is I'm supposed to be working on that day—words eventually begin to flow, and those words, written in a fog of pain and anesthetic, often surprise me. I don't know from what part of my subconscious they emanate, or what normal brain barriers have been temporarily dismantled to make room for the endorphin flow, but often—not always mind you, but often enough—the words, the ideas, the imagery, the revelations, are those that weren't finding a way onto the page on previous pain-free mornings. I find myself typing those hidden truths one sometimes just blurts out when not thinking too hard, the things I didn't know I knew.

These little gems of sentences, phrases, ideas, or whatever are crude, unformed, desperate for revision—but they are usually alive, worth spending time with, peculiar in a good way. They are the surprises that keep a piece of writing going.

Try it.

It hurts. 🐦

Dinty W. Moore

Editor of *Brevity: A Journal of Concise Literary Nonfiction*, Dinty W. Moore is also author of two books of nonfiction, *The Accidental Buddhist* and *The Emperor's Virtual Clothes*, both from Algonquin Books, and a collection of stories, *Toothpick Men*.

His fiction and essays have appeared in *The New York Times Magazine*, *The Georgia Review*, *Fourth Genre*, *The Utne Reader*, and numerous other journals and magazines.

Dinty teaches writing at Penn State Altoona and has authored a creative writing textbook, *The Truth of the Matter: Art and Craft in Creative Nonfiction*.

Teeth Gnashing

by Dan Wakefield

In his classic essay "Politics and the English Language," George Orwell gives a list of rules of writing. All writers who fail to follow these rules should be stripped of their laptops. My favorite rule is: "Never use a long word where a short word will do." I would like to keep that one set in stone and also add a subrule to it in the same spirit: Never use a pretentious word where a plain one will do.

This added rule was suggested to me when my esteemed fellow writer Bruce Jay Friedman told me why he could not continue in his effort to read *The Da Vinci Code*. Friedman explained he could plow through the turgid text no further when he read that the protagonist "donned" his bathrobe. After a deservedly word-weary sigh, Friedman explained that "*Emperors* 'don' their bathrobe. Regular people just put it on."

After the ban on pretentious and/or pompous words I would order a rule against the use of the … ellipsis. The use of the mysterious three dots is a favorite among writing students, especially the "sensitive" variety. The definition of *ellipsis* in my *American Heritage College Dictionary* is "the omission of a word or phrase necessary for a complete syntactical construction but not necessary for understanding." It is commonly and erroneously used, however, to indicate the author's belief that something tremendously significant is going on, something that can't be … expressed … in ordinary words. Something like this:

"He looked deeply into her eyes. … Then he turned away."

My colleague at Florida International University, Lynn Barrett, told me this kind of misuse was usually employed to give the writing a certain … "waftiness."

Exactly!

Okay, *waftiness* is not a word—but it should be.

The writer who injects waftiness into his manuscript is likely to feel the necessity of using words far more "expressive" than the word *said*, as in: "*Pass the salt*," *she said*. How pedestrian is a character who merely *says*. Let her—or him—regardless of gender, race, or religion, *expostulate*, *opine*, *aver*, *lament*, or even, as a last resort, *reply*, but never simply *say*, as in he *said*.

The writer who requires his characters to expostulate, opine, aver, and lament is probably also the writer who forgets to observe the most

After the ban on pretentious and/or pompous words I would order a rule against the use of the ... ellipsis.

basic rule of manners: Introduce someone new. The aspiring writer might, to her or his eternal benefit, read every essay written by George Orwell and notice (among other things) that every time a new person is introduced into the narrative, he or she is *introduced*. We are given a sense of what the person looks like, or sounds like, or maybe even smells like, so we have some notion of who we are reading about. Nothing is more rude to the reader than to bring a

new person into the story by name only, as in:

> When Jane saw Joe walk into the room, her blood pressure spiked. She was overcome with love and lust. After exchanging a few comments about the weather, she followed him from the room in a trance of passion.

But who is this Joe? Is he fat or thin, blonde or bald, dressed as a count or a cowboy? *Is* he a count or a cowboy? All we

were told was his name, and it may be pages later—if ever—that we get to know what he looks like, sounds like, acts like, and what it was about him that made him fatally attractive to Jane.

People who would never be so rude as to bring someone to a party and fail to introduce him to the rest of the guests sometimes forget to introduce the people they are writing about to the reader. The reader is, after all—or should be—the guest of honor at any story.

Is there any way to stop these barbaric practices? Certainly! Perpetrators should be put in chains, fed only tofu, and not allowed sleep, while teams of Russian holy men read them, in endless rotation, *The Elements of Style* by Strunk and White. ❧

Dan Wakefield

Novelist, journalist, and screenwriter Dan Wakefield is writer-in-residence at Florida International University.

His best-selling novels *Going All the Way* and *Starting Over* were produced as feature films, and a documentary film has been produced of his memoir *New York in the Fifties*. His nonfiction books on spirituality include *Returning: A Spiritual Journey*, *Creating From the Spirit*, *The Story of Your Life: Writing a Spiritual Autobiography*, *Expect a Miracle*, and *How Do We Know When It's God?: A Spiritual Memoir*.

You Really Don't Have Anything Better to Do

by Robert Olen Butler

Your fingernails do not have to be clipped until after the day's production of words is done.

This includes your thumbs, by the way. It is a corollary of the uber-rule-of-thumb: Write every day. That's a painful thing, if you are striving to create art from the welter of your unconscious, the usual place art comes from. So when you sit down each day to do this thing, your natural defense mechanisms—whose wise job it is to keep you out of that place—start suggesting alternate, more pressing lines of endeavor. Don't write, clip your nails. Clean the toilets. Get a six-month head start on organizing the deductible receipts for your taxes. Anything. One of the most insidious is: Read a good book. Which is often simply an invitation to hide in somebody else's voice and vision of the world so you don't have to do the frankly terrifying work of speaking your own to that blank page. ❦

Robert Olen Butler

Robert Olen Butler is the author of ten novels and three collections of stories; his work has received The Pulitzer Prize, a National Magazine Award, and the Richard and Hilda Rosenthal Award from the American Academy and Institute of Arts and Letters.

Divine Reading—Holy Writing

by Melanie Rae Thon

Michel Foucault says: "One writes in order to become other than what one is." My wise friend Mark Robbins once asked me, "Isn't that what prayer is, the dedicated concentration of your being on that which will help you become the person you know you should be?"

I have two "rules" for my own work: Strive to be as patient as a monk; hope to remain as curious as a child.

The editors of *The Desert Fathers* describe *lectio divina* (divine or spiritual reading) as the meditative approach "by which the reader seeks to taste and savor the beauty and truth of every phrase and passage." There are four steps: reading, meditating, resting in the sense of God's nearness, and, ultimately, resolving to govern one's actions in the light of new understanding. This kind of reading—devotion to spiritual inquiry and the desire to be enlightened, even transfigured, by what we read—is an act of prayer.

> *This kind of reading—devotion to spiritual inquiry and the desire to be enlightened, even transfigured, by what we read—is an act of prayer.*

I believe that *writing* can be *holy*, just as *reading* can be *spiritual*. As a person, I wish "to taste and savor the beauty and truth" of every experience; as a writer I must do my best to render it, to give it back through language and hope to spark one reader's memory and imagination. I hope, as Thich Nhat Hanh says, "to offer joy to one person each morning, and relieve the grief of one person each afternoon."

The longing to do justice to the thing I am trying to describe is, for me, a way of resting in the sense of God's nearness. But even if you are not one who contemplates God as you try to understand and evoke the human adventure, surely all who write (or think or feel) must pause a thousand times a day in wonder. It's amazing we don't burst apart with the sheer rapture of sensation buzzing through us: sun on skin, smell of cedar, splash of red so dark and deep it makes me dizzy. Julian of Norwich says, "Pain is transient, bliss eternal." When I awaken

myself, when I cease to judge experience as good or bad and simply marvel at its intensity, I know sweet Julian is right: the Kingdom is here, on earth, waiting for us to step into it.

Ansel Adams says: "I believe in beauty—I believe in stories and water and air and soil—people and their future and their fate." If we believe in these things, then the love and patience required to evoke them for our readers becomes sacred. Art *is* an affirmation of life—not only of our separate lives, but of our lives within the endless body of all living things, our lives as they are connected to stones and clouds and wolves and spiders.

Faith-full immersion in the prayer of writing sometimes leads me to country I have not known. In the borderlands, I hear violin and flute and drum, each separate sound. Even when the music stops, vibrations sing through my bones. This is love, the place where I become other than myself—not one, but all—the interlude where I am quiet enough to feel compassion for someone from whom I have been estranged, or of whom I have been fearful. Calm at last, I enter the mystery of a family's grief to become each person's witness. I am not afraid; I am restored moment by moment. I see a pattern of light in fluttering leaves and feel the extravagance of God's love roar into me. Jim Corbett says: "The love of God *is* God's love." He means there is no separation between *loving* and being *loved*: As our love for all creation spills out, the recognition that we *are* loved flows back into us. The Sufi poet Hafiz says: "The Beloved with His own hands is tending, / Raising like a precious child, / Himself in / You." It is our challenge and our bliss to live as if we believe this.

From this place of peace, I "resolve to govern [my] actions in the light of new understanding," to be kinder, quieter, more amazed, more merciful. Hafiz whispers: "Everyone / is God speaking / Why not be polite and / Listen to him?" Meister Eckhart reminds me: "Apprehend God in all things. Every single creature is full of God and is a book about God. Every creature is a Word of God."

I surrender. When I am free of fear, I long to touch, to know; I am filled with endless gratitude. I believe (for a moment or an hour) it might be possible to transcend my former limits. I see that writing is a path to become other than what I am.

But it never lasts! I fail and fail. And so I must return to my practice, the prayer of writing, the passion of loving attention to each thing as I am trying

76

to describe it: the green flannel shirt, the swirling crows, my father's wild roses. I write to stay awake to stay alive. I rise before dawn and return to the word with childlike wonder.

And so I remind myself—again and forever—

> Do what thou hast in hand with perfect dignity, and feeling of affection, and freedom, and justice, and to give thyself relief from all other thoughts.
>
> —Marcus Aurelius 🐞

Melanie Rae Thon

Melanie Rae Thon's most recent books are *First, Body* and *Sweet Hearts*. She teaches at the University of Utah and lives in migration between Montana, Washington, Utah, and Arizona. In 1996, *Granta* named her one of America's best young novelists.

Names 'n' Such

by Robert Rosenblum

When people talk of rules, they often say they have been *guided* by them. My own belief is that rules, for writers, are false guides and should, to whatever extent possible, be kept out of one's mind. There are two, however, that were passed along to me by other writers of fiction and have taken root to the extent that they always intrude into the process whenever they might apply.

The more useless and absurd of the two was mentioned by a writer who had the same agent as I did, and with whom I became friendly. Looking over something I had given him to read in an early stage, he came across the word *such*, and said that the word *such*—as in *it was such a shame*—should always be avoided. It was, he said, invariably a weak substitute for qualifiers that could be more specific and thoughtful. It may simply be because this dictum was delivered with such authority that I resolved at that point to do everything possible to avoid ever using the word *such* again. The writer who gave me this advice was (and not too long after) sued for plagiarism, and subsequently gave up writing fiction at all to work exclusively in television—where plagiarism seems not only to be common, but practically worshipped. So perhaps he was not someone to be heeded. Nevertheless, to this day, although I have sometimes found it unavoidable to use the word *such*—hey, it works!—I always feel a pang of guilt when I do. Such is life.

The second rule was told to me by an English writer, and by the very fact of his literary heritage I gave it even more weight. It also came to

Be very careful in choosing the names of your characters, for this will help to make them who they are.

me when I was in the midst of my first attempt at writing fiction, and was thus immediately influential. The rule is to be very careful in choosing the names of your characters, for this will help to make them who they are. I have found this rule to be of crucial value every time I write a book. How many times do you have to write that name from first page to last? It has to be real to you every time it appears in front of your eyes. Incidentally, the chap who gave me this rule later committed suicide after a period when he was having difficulty with his writing. And

I wonder if he was just having trouble coming up with the right names.

Anyway, dear reader, beware what you find here. It's not impossible that some genuinely absurd bit of advice—if not more than one—will lodge in your brain and haunt you from time to time as you sit before the page. On the other hand, all these roadblocks to convention—other people's conventions, rules of any kind—may only block the road to the ordinary, and force you to take the fork to discovery and invention. 🐛

Robert Rosenblum

Robert Rosenblum is the author of thirty-six novels in multiple genres, most written under pseudonyms (including female bestsellers), a device to which he attributes his good luck—thus far—in escaping writer's block.

Laissez-Faire Writing

by Karen Brennan

I don't know if I'm a rule o' thumb kind of gal. I'm not that OCD. I don't arrange the pens on my desk in a pattern, nor do I have the need to wear a special bathrobe before embarking on the creative journey in front of my computer. And when it comes to the work itself, I am a little laissez-faire: You write, it either sucks or thrills you, you can either work on it or not. I take a lot of naps.

Nonetheless, I have managed to plumb my shallows for a rule o' thumb, which is this: Write for pleasure, your own. When it (the work, the page, the words) stops delivering—when the muscles go slack at the jaw, when the eyes wander to the window of dull sky, when the mouth craves chocolate—put it aside. And if, when you return, the whole enterprise seems like just too much drudgery and

You write, it either sucks or thrills you, you can either work on it or not. I take a lot of naps.

pain, that's all the sign I need to abandon the thing and move on to something more nourishing, like a trip to the mall.

This is, of course, counter to everything I've been taught about success and Americanism. It is the lazy girl way—it reveals my poor character. And also, p.s., it doesn't work at the gym. ❦

Karen Brennan

A professor at the University of Arizona, Karen Brennan is the author of *Wild Desire* and *The Garden in Which I Walk*, both fiction, and a memoir, *Being With Rachel: A Story of Memory and Survival*, as well as two collections of poetry. Brennan is the recipient of the AWP Award in Fiction and a National Endowment for the Arts fellowship. She is a regular faculty member of the Warren Wilson MFA Program for Writers.

Pay Attention

by Scott Russell Sanders

When aspiring writers ask me for advice, and we have only a few minutes or a few lines to share, here is the gist of what I say.

Write by ear, not by rules. To do that well, your ear must be trained, which means you should listen carefully to language in conversation and stories and songs, as well as on the page. If you've forgotten how sensuous language is, how captivating, how musical, spend time with a toddler who's learning to speak. Linger where people talk vividly—a job site, farmers market, courtroom, coffee house, union hall—and write down what you hear.

Read widely and patiently. Read the best works you can find, not only by your contemporaries but also by your predecessors. When a passage or a word appeals to you, underline it, say it over to yourself, copy it down. When you are moved by a piece of writing, examine how it is made—from the fine details of diction and syntax to the overall structure and tone—and then try adapting to your own work the features you admire.

With rare exceptions, the language used on television is laced with clichés, subservient to visual images, and enslaved to sponsors. So if you wish to avoid dulling your ear and filling your mind with hackneyed story lines, shun the glowing tube.

In preparing to write, search for questions that haunt you, experiences that fascinate you, instead of ones that are fashionable or easy. Good writing is a way of discovering what you don't already know, or of clarifying what you only dimly perceive. The claim that Flannery O'Connor made about fiction holds true for all kinds of writing: No surprise in the writer, no surprise in the reader.

The point of writing is not to see your work in print, although nearly everyone who writes hopes to be published. The point of writing is to make something skillfully and beautifully out of words, to discern some of your own heart's truths, and to speak memorably to strangers.

Writing is one side of a conversation; reading is the other. So bear your readers in mind. Consider where they might stumble, where they might disagree. Never trick them; never try to force your judgments on them. Ask yourself, line by line, what readers need to know in order to follow your story, feel your emotion, share your discoveries, and then answer those needs. This is not a matter of coddling, but of courtesy.

Don't confuse obscurity with mystery. Obscurity in writing can be cleared up, because it results from the author's lack of skill or care; mystery belongs to the nature of things. Don't create trivial puzzles by withholding information, leaving out connections, or muddling exposition. Save your readers' attention for the genuine puzzles, those aspects of our lives and our cosmic home that we do not understand.

Don't confuse violence with significance. While there is plenty of violence in the world, from sidewalk muggings to wide-scale war, don't introduce bloodshed or menace into your writing merely for an emotional charge. To be meaningful, violence must be given context, a history; otherwise, it is a substitute for imagination.

Don't show off by cloaking plain ideas in fancy words. Avoid jargon, because it excludes many readers. When only specialized terms will do, explain what they

mean. So far as possible, use common language, because in doing so you enrich and renew our shared understanding.

Don't strike poses, especially those of the bored intellectual, unappreciated genius, or cynical sophisticate. Cynicism and irony are cheap, and they often mask a fear of taking responsibility for one's words.

Remember the body. Appeal to the senses—all of them, including touch and taste and smell. Even in making abstract arguments, be concrete whenever possible. "No ideas but in things," William Carlos Williams remarked: Our minds cling to the tangible stuff of the world.

Don't strike poses, especially those of the bored intellectual, unappreciated genius, or cynical sophisticate. Cynicism and irony are cheap, and they often mask a fear of taking responsibility for one's words.

Remember the planet. Every human experience occurs somewhere on Earth, inside or outside a building, in city or town or countryside. So ground your writing in place, and not just in the ether of language.

Remember other species. It's natural for us to be intrigued by our own kind. But humans are only one among millions of species on Earth, all riding this globe around the sun. We evolved within that abundance, intimate with animals and plants. To keep faith with our past, spend time outdoors, and in the wilds if you can reach them. Out of respect for the living web that supports us, make room in your writing for some of our fellow creatures.

If your ideas are going to stay with us, we need containers to hold them. So tell stories. Use examples. Create a speaking voice that lingers in our ears after we close the book. Find metaphors that link one fragment of experience with another. Give us patterns, either those you discover or those you invent. When patterns on the page coincide with patterns in the world, we experience the result as beauty.

If you mean to write well, then aim to write every day, as you would practice a musical instrument or train for a sport or pursue a profession. Keep a journal. Send letters. Take notes. Write in your head, translating life's unbroken flow into words.

Ultimately, life slips between words, overflows the containers we make. The work of writing becomes most difficult and most rewarding at the frontiers of the sayable, where language reaches out from the known to the unknown. However skillful we may become in using language, we should never forget that the universe is grander and more subtle than anything we can say about it.

To realize, moment by moment, the depth and wonder of existence is the goal of artistic practice, as it is of spiritual practice. So wake up. Be mindful. Pay attention. This is the key not only to good writing but to good living. 🐛

Scott Russell Sanders

Scott Russell Sanders teaches at Indiana University, among limestone hills never bulldozed by glaciers, and he writes books, the latest of which is *A Private History of Awe*, a memoir of his lifelong spiritual search.

Scott Russell Sanders' many publications include novels, collections of short stories, works of creative nonfiction, as well as books for children. His writing appears regularly in *The Georgia Review*, *Orion*, *Audubon*, and numerous anthologies. He has been awarded fellowships from the Guggenheim Foundation, the National Endowment for the Arts, and the Lilly Endowment. Sanders' work has also received the AWP Award in Creative Nonfiction and the Kenyon Review Award for Literary Excellence.

Susan Neville's Secret Rule

by Pablo Medina

I was reading a volume of Pliny the Younger's letters on a terrazza overlooking Lake Como when I found, in letter LXVII to his friend Macer, the anecdote of a woman of Como whose husband had been afflicted for some time with an ulcer "in those parts that modesty conceals." The woman finally convinced her husband to let her see the sore, after which she gave him her honest opinion that it was, in fact, incurable. She then advised him that he should put an end to his life, for what good is a man with chancre on his masculinity? She was, however, famous for her devotion, and seeing that her husband hesitated in doing what needed to be done, she tied herself to him and plunged first into the lake, dragging him with her.

I was so troubled by this story that I dropped the book and ran inside to the nearest powder room, where I exposed myself and checked carefully "those parts that modesty conceals." Once I assured myself that I was healthy and that there wasn't the least blemish on me that might induce my wife to recommend a premature end to my life, I went back outside and continued reading the letters, some of which Pliny had written from the same promontory where I was now sitting. The rest of the afternoon passed uneventfully. At seven I met my wife for drinks in the garden with the other guests. At seven-thirty, as was the custom in the villa, we dined on *trota di lago*, *polenta fritta trei formaggi*, and a succulent *asparagi con uovo*, all staples of the area. The wine was excellent, a well-balanced Barolo that tasted angelic, and the dessert most delicate, a *crema al cioccolato con pinoli*. The fine dinner, the presence of my beloved wife, and the company of good friends, however, did not allay my anxiety. The rest of the night I spent unable to sleep and dawn found me thinking about that poor man's privates and his devoted wife's sacrifice.

As the sun rose over Cisalpine Gaul I determined that I would never write about the awful afflictions that Pliny had so casually referred to in his letter and that had caused me such unease, nor would any of the characters of my stories and novels so despair as to cause the death, not of one but of two otherwise admirable and loving people. Moreover, it became my goal to expunge any allusion to penile pustules, no matter how veiled or circumspect, I came across in my readings. I started in my own library, buying a thick marker for the purpose, blacking out the offending passages until all the books I owned had been cleansed of the demeaning references. I continued with my friends' books. When invited to their homes, I sat by their bookshelves while they feasted and drank and used my marker with the moral ferocity of a Torquemada. I worked with stealth and diligence and so was never discovered.

My success gave me the courage to enter the public and university libraries of my city. I exhausted the ink of dozens of markers in the process and almost exhausted myself until I came to realize that this was not a job for one man but for an army of men (and women). I found a few others whose concerns equaled mine and we founded a secret society, the American Society of Prepuce Preservers, or ASPP for short. Our motto is "We are many, we are driven, we are troubled." Given the secretive nature of the group, I am not allowed to divulge how many members belong or where they reside. Suffice it to say that only three people showed up at our first meeting, including a homeless man who came for

It became my goal to expunge any allusion to penile pustules, no matter how veiled or circumspect, I came across in my readings.

the cookies and punch I served. Since that time our membership has grown steadily and resolutely. We have sent representatives to other cities and countries who have opened chapters of our organization against the objections of local opponents, who mock us and call us Anti-Plinysts (Antiplinistas overseas).

When next you see a person with a black marker in his (or her) hand and a determined look in his (or her) eyes, greet that person and thank him (or her) for his (or her) labors. We are many, we are driven, we are troubled. It is only a matter of time before we prevail. 🐛

Pablo Medina

After living in Havana, Cuba, for the first twelve years of his life, Pablo Medina moved with his family to New York City, where his culture shock was softened by snow and countless visits to the New York Public Library. He is the author of four poetry collections, three novels, a memoir, and a book of translations. Medina has received several awards for his work, among them grants from the Lila Wallace–Reader's Digest Fund, the National Endowment for the Arts, and the Rockefeller Foundation. He is on the writing faculties of the New School University and Warren Wilson College.

The Great I-Am
by Brian Kiteley

I used *I* as rarely as I could in my first novel, *Still Life With Insects*, even though the book was told from a first-person point of view. My grandfather was the model for the main character in the book, and he spoke without much reference to himself in conversations and even in his own stories about himself. This restriction of the first-person pronoun seemed crucial to capturing his persona on paper. When I first started teaching, I wrote up an exercise to play with this idea, and the exercise remains in the book that rose out of these workshop exercises (*The 3 A.M. Epiphany*). The exercise suggests students write a first-person fragment of fiction that is six hundred words long using the first-person pronoun only three times. This difficult and artificial restraint should make writers aware of all the other operations that go into a narrative that is told by someone, other than the voice and self.

The Language poets (who practiced poetry against the model of the Confessional poets of the 1950s and 1960s) had a horror of the *I*. As beautiful, groundbreaking, and politically and linguistically adventurous as Language poetry was, it sometimes became solipsistic in the opposite way that the great Confessional poems by Lowell and Sexton were. Solipsism is the theory that the self is the only object of real knowledge or the only thing that really exists. No one can deny this, technically, because we are locked in ourselves, and proof of anyone else's existence is circumstantial. Writing is perhaps the only proof there is of the existence of someone other than ourselves.

William Vollmann says, "We should never write without feeling. Unless we are much more interesting than we imagine we are, we should strive to feel not only about Self, but also about Other. ... We must treat Self and Other as equal partners." The Self in fiction is the given, and the Other is the icing on the cake—humor is possible only with two or more characters. Tragedy deals with individuals, and comedy with classes of people. We want fiction to explore someone else's consciousness—we read fiction to feel the way someone

Young writers should use the I sparingly. We should look outside ourselves, beyond our own small worlds. We can imagine a larger space than we usually do.

else feels. The philosopher Charles Taylor says a "human being alone is an impossibility. ... Outside of the continuing conversation of a community, which provides the language by which we draw our background distinctions, human agency ... would be not just impossible, but inconceivable." Young writers should use the *I* sparingly. We should look outside ourselves, beyond our own small worlds. We can imagine a larger space than we usually do.

I used to write journals—I have maybe two thousand pages of these formerly blank books. The early journals are tedious reading. The Self crowds out practically anything else, and I find myself shouting at that twenty-year-old, "Let me see around this huge immoveable object to the interesting stories you're not telling." Eventually, I did become bored with my own dramas, and I began to observe the world around me, listening to other people's voices and watching their gestures. A solid, helpful Self is vital to a good piece of fiction, but at the same time all fiction is built on unreliable narratives. I've heard that the late Frank Conroy ordered his students not to use unreliable narrators in his Iowa workshops. We're all unreliable, but this fickle mind that always guides us through a piece of fiction can be made more useful, if not more reliable.

In the commentary on this exercise in *The 3 A.M. Epiphany*, I tell an old joke: A guy at a party is talking to a woman for a long while. He says, "Enough about me, what do *you* think of me?" There is certainly room for boors like this in fiction, but great fiction is told by the woman who walks away from this man, when she describes him to her girlfriend, laughing at his ridiculousness, but also finding something touching beyond his mere egotism: the way he fiddles with the corners of his shirt collar. She guesses that when he was a child, his mother called the corners of his favorite pillow Matthew, Mark, Luke, and John—residue of his mother's own religious youth. Somehow these biblical names reassure this man-child, and he repeats them to himself as he's playing with his collar points (stand-ins for this favorite pillow). All his shirts are eventually ruined at the collar points, she tells her girlfriend, who marvels at the way this woman sees into the heart of even the dimmest soul. ❦

Brian Kiteley

Brian Kiteley, director of the Ph.D. program in creative writing at the University of Denver, is the author of *The 3 A.M. Epiphany*, a book of fiction exercises, and the novels *Still Life With Insects* and *I Know Many Songs, But I Cannot Sing.*

Never Write About Writing

by R.M. Berry

My cubicle is of determined proportions, a simple matter of increments, even if I've yet to recount them all. It was yesterday, or some time before, that, having ventured to my usual extremes, I came nose-up on this cranny where the ceiling and a partition joined. Their intersection made a line hardly different from others, slender, depthless, but no sooner did I remark it than I felt myself being drawn. This seam, you'll understand, signified nothing in itself, a mere length, but since two surfaces had aligned there, made an edge so to speak, it seemed to insinuate some limit, a shape. Was my workspace other than I'd imagined? I wondered. My quandary stopped short of reflection, mind you, but I didn't immediately return to my senses.

I knew how to follow out a line, this way to a beginning, that to an end, assuming of course what appeared straight wasn't in reality a circle, but I could see that the seam led nowhere, was simply a meeting of perpendicular planes. What had drawn me must lie beyond it, I reasoned, as if the ceiling and partition formed not so much a conjunction as a border. Needless to say, this prospect had its preposterous side, since what I'm calling a line was more precisely a crevice. I mean, no one had inscribed a mark on my cubicle, said in effect *this far, no further*, or no one but its manufacturer. In all literalness, my container had no portion of itself, no inner recess or outer void which, merely by going over the edge, I could hope to reach. I don't mean to say I'd never ventured outside it, hadn't visited Vermont, bought groceries, bathed. I'm hardly a soul. But within was where I'd always worked, made of myself all I'd become, and so this comeuppance now was alarming. It was as though what had seemed everything to me was

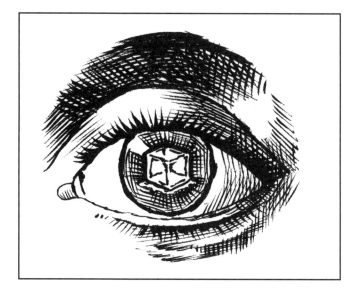

Ah, the past! That was what my cubicle lacked, as though I couldn't tell what my own container signified, not because its lines were hard to make out, but because they'd never been other than presently.

only everything in a manner of speaking, was partial to others, or truncated. I found myself wanting—and the experience felt utterly new—to imagine a world "without" my cubicle.

I have little or no idea what I'm saying. I was aware of the complications all about me, the plots on-going, bedlam at every turn, and although my workspace seemed one speck amid a vastness, that was hardly reason to fixate on this line, to not get on with everything. But having intuited some beyond, I found it no small matter now just to forget. I mean, even if all I could imagine were in a sense already here, did that make the unimaginable no place?

I drew closer. At such proximity the line appeared less like a seam or fissure than a kind of shadow, two refractions of light, one reflecting less acutely on my viewpoint than the other. While the ceiling absorbed most of its illumination, the wall seemed a veritable mirror, sending every flash of brilliance directly back. I couldn't tell what to make of this difference. I continued contemplating it for what seemed the longest period, hoping that, if I were sufficiently still, sufficiently alert, the secret of my workspace would reveal itself in time, but as I struggled to keep my two sides in focus, I realized with a start that I had misplaced my spectacles. This seemed a perilous lapse. A cubicle even at its most thrilling is far from sensational, but without spectacles it can appear genuinely dull. If ever I descend to narrating, God help me. I might as well be a poet! Anyway, words occurred to me then, something to the effect that, if I hoped to surpass my limit, I'd need my old device, those lenses through which I'd always looked at everything, and even to my mind's myopic eye, this truth had the bedazzling self-evidence of an inspiration.

Well, it seemed a trivial matter, having once been thus inspired, to be inspired again, so I waited for the whereabouts of my spectacles to occur to me. However, they never materialized. I would've happily distracted myself with almost any catastrophe, the collapse of some despotic regime or a Kansas farm boy's heartbreak, but my ceiling and wall refused to come together as my spectacles had done in the past. Ah, the past! *That* was what my cubicle lacked, as though I couldn't tell what my own container signified, not because its lines were hard to make out, but because they'd never been other than presently. Some might be bored by this, but I found it riveting. A significance right there

on my surface had always appeared beyond me. Were I to recount it, I couldn't simply do as before, since what had limited my workspace must've been my doing in the first place. No, what wanted recounting now seemed like my childhood or skin, a reality that, even if I'd lived in utter ignorance of it, no one else could've known more intimately than I. So there I remained, wits on edge, not a word to say, but feeling strangely liberated. Without doubt, some will consider this a catastrophe itself, and I don't mean to deny them. After all, what has my cubicle to do with denial? And yet it wasn't as if I could imagine my workspace any longer. I'd been comprised, for God's sake! This was me! So I returned to my line, a seeming accident, and vowed to let my senses have their way. There'd been a task, I recalled, an object forming. Where had I left off? No telling. ❧

R.M. Berry

R.M. Berry, professor of English at Florida State University, is author of the novel *Leonardo's Horse*, and the story collections *Dictionary of Modern Anguish* and *Plane Geometry and Other Affairs of the Heart.*

Sage Advice From an Acknowledged Master of the Form

by Robin Hemley

I don't read fiction because it's a waste of time.

In nonfiction, there's a contract between writer and reader.

It's okay to alter facts as long as you tell an emotional truth.

There's no such thing as objective truth anyway.

What about the Holocaust memoir written by someone who never experienced the Holocaust?

What *is* the relation between reality TV and reality?

Memoirists are self-indulgent whiners.

Fiction writers hide behind a cloak of invention.

It doesn't matter what's invented and what really happened.

What about *The Education of Little Tree*, an "autobiography" of a Native American kid written by a KKK member?

God loves irony.

But it matters to me. If I walk out of this room and discover that the author wasn't a member of the KKK, I'll hold it against you forever.

That's why we have libel laws.

Facts are facts.

Facts are always in dispute.

History is always disputed.

Custer was a hero.

Manifest Destiny made this country great.

I'm sick of all of these tales of abuse and neglect.

Slavery wasn't all that bad.

I hate confession.

I hate the self-importance of writers.

Most wisdom is received wisdom.

Six million? Maybe it was only 5,999,999.

Don't trivialize the Holocaust.

Everyone is always telling me I should write my story.

Anne Frank stands in for all the six million.

Otto Frank expunged passages from Anne's diary that spoke of sexuality.

It's a true story.

What does that mean?

It could have happened.

I'm afraid it will hurt my mother.

That's my story, not yours.

What matters is how it's ordered, the way it's told, not the content.

You're invading my privacy.

    I'm an artiste!

      Memory always lies.

      Money talks and bullshit walks.

      Who's to say what really happened?

        You can't make up scenes and characters and call that nonfiction.

          But it really happened!

          The lines are always blurred.

          If all nonfiction must be true, then must all fiction be false?

96

Boy, if someone told *my* story, no one would believe it.

I don't care. It's boring/stupid/clumsy.

Stranger than fiction.

What right do you have to tell my story?

I'm just the narrator, lady. You'll have to talk to the author. He's away from his desk. May I put you on hold? ❦

Robin Hemley

Robin Hemley is the author of seven books of fiction and nonfiction and is the director of the nonfiction writing program at the University of Iowa. His awards for his fiction include The Nelson Algren Award from *The Chicago Tribune*, the Hugh J. Luke Award from *Prairie Schooner*, two Pushcart Prizes, and many others. He is a graduate of the Iowa Writers Workshop and was editor of the *Bellingham Review* for five years.

Write Short Chapters Whenever Possible

by Joey Goebel

Short chapters are well-suited for those modern readers who can't miss a second of their favorite reality shows.

I fear that the idea of sitting down and reading a book is becoming increasingly archaic in our point-and-click computerized culture. Technology has made instant gratification the only way of life our youngest generations have known. But as of this writing, no one has figured out a way to download a novel into a reader's brain. We still have to read the old-fashioned way, word by word, sentence by sentence, paragraph by paragraph, chapter by chapter.

But just in case the readers of the future won't have the patience for the antiquated process of reading a novel, I abide by a simple rule that gives my writing an exaggerated sense of movement: I make chapters as short as possible, sometimes half a page.

I realize this is no innovation. I first witnessed the method in Kurt Vonnegut's 1963 masterpiece *Cat's Cradle*, in which most of the 127 chapters last a page and a half. Such short chapters are well-suited for those modern readers who can't miss a second of their favorite reality shows. After all, an entire chapter could be read during each commercial break.

Having one- to two-page chapters enhances a novel's tempo. For instance, if I'm writing a long scene, I often divide it into several chapters. That way, I can end each little chapter with a punch that drives a point home for the reader, a pithy snap that provides the aforementioned instant gratification. This breaks the monotony of a long scene, and it is surely appreciated by those members of my audience with short attention spans.

But is this a method of dumbing down a novel? I don't think so. More than anything else, it's a typographical trick. The actual content of the scene need not be trimmed of a single

word, and the elements of the story are unaffected. Ultrashort chapters are merely a more reader-friendly way of presenting this content on paper. With the blank space and chapter numbers (or headings) oc-

curring between each chapter, the reader constantly feels as though he or she is getting somewhere. And catering to a twenty-first-century reader's needs isn't what I'd call an offense. I'd call it a necessity. ❧

Joey Goebel

Joey Goebel is author of *The Anomalies* (a Book-Sense pick) and *Torture the Artist*, both published by MacAdam/Cage. Goebel's protagonists are intelligent rebels, sensible madmen, and rejected dreamers disgusted by a society that embraces Justin Timberlake. Goebel lives in Henderson, Kentucky.

Dixon's Rules

by Stephen Dixon

Never write a fiction where a character is named Molly Bloom, Becky Sharpe, James Joyce, Count Tolstoy, or Stephen. Never even have a character with the initials S.D., K., S., or Z.

Never write a fiction with a character running around in a gorilla suit, not anything with a character suffering from bulimia, anorexia, gastric reflux, diarrhea, or hemorrhoids.

Never write a scene where a needle or some sharp object

Never use the word soul *in a piece of prose that refers to the animating and vital principle in human beings, credited with the faculties of thought, action, and emotion, and often conceived of as an immaterial entity.*

goes into an eye, or where the eye is damaged seriously in any way. Testicles are also out.

Also go for the simplest word in your prose; eliminate sesquipedalianism and lexiphanicism.

Never use the word *soul* in a piece of prose that refers to the animating and vital principle in human beings, credited with the faculties of thought, action, and emotion, and often conceived of as an immaterial entity. Also, never take the exact words out of a dictionary when you want to define a word or term in your writing.

Never title a story or novel *War and Peace, Crime and Punishment, The Master and Margarita*. It is okay, though, to title a fiction *Crime and Peace, War and Margarita, The Master and Punishment*, or any variation of those.

Never write with a mug of tea or coffee near the finished manuscript. Always make sure your hands are dry before you tear the finished manuscript page out of the typewriter. Never tear a finished manuscript page out of a typewriter.

Never use the word *fallacious* more than once in any fiction, no matter how long. If you have to use it once, make sure it's used in dialog and that the character who speaks it is a fop. Don't have any fops in your fiction.

Never learn the definition of iambic pentemeter or even the correct spelling of the term.

Never write a fiction with a male stripper or nun in it.

From now on, avoid writing any fiction where the narrator's father is a dentist, the mother was a beauty queen, the wife is seriously ill, and the narrator has two children and both are daughters. Don't ever write about twins, either. ❧

Stephen Dixon

Stephen Dixon is the author of twenty-one books of fiction, two of them finalists for the National Book Award, and has published more than four hundred short stories. He has been recognized with a grant from the National Endowment for the Arts, a Guggenheim Fellowship, the Pushcart Prize, an O. Henry Award and by the American Academy and Institute for Arts and Letters.

Big Dogs and Little Dogs
by T.M. McNally

Rule is a clever word: it manages the kingdom; it measures the length along the page, or width. Begin, always, with the word.

The opposable thumb, I'm told, is what set humankind down the evolutionary path toward dominion. Generally speaking, I prefer myth—Adam, Eve, a crafty serpent; or a pretty girl and dark underlord, and a pomegranate—to elucidate the great mysteries, but I take the scientist's point. And I know other species have language—whales, for example, sing, and apes will eagerly give to one the bird—but no other species have, I think, poetry. Or myth.

"Imagination is All," wrote William Blake. That is as good a rule I know. A tenet of my faith.

In the manner of P.D. Eastman's *Go Dog. Go!* I think there are big dogs and little dogs. Big rules and little rules. The little ones tend to yap, the big ones, woof. Both will be equally inclined to bite or protect you and your loved ones from the dark.

Literary fiction does not sell—that is a little rule.

Never confuse the fact of publication with the written word upon the page—that is a big rule.

Nobody reads anymore—that is a little rule.

Write what you want to read—that is a big rule.

Write what you want to read. The more you read, the wider your tastes, the vaster your literary sensibility, the greater your intellectual adventures. That is to say, the more you read, the more you bring to the table when it's time for fellowship and conversation.

You'll note I'm advising you not to write what you think others want to read.

Fuck 'em. Nobody reads anyway.

One of the most irritating platitudes I can think of goes like this: Show, don't tell.

Gag me with a PC, or a creative writing workshop.

Tell anything you like. The secret is to tell me—your reader, yourself—something you do not know, and conveying that secret gracefully will involve the act of discovery. Surprise. A positively honest exploration of the interiors of the human heart.

You may say anything you like so long as what you say is useful to the life of the mind. Detail is meaningful only in context. But detail in and of

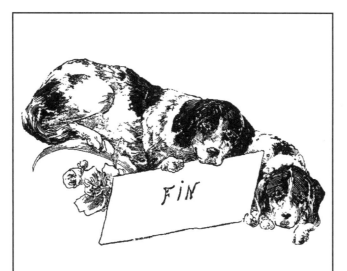

itself is not interesting. A rock. A dog. A splinter in the brain.

What makes the detail meaningful is the contextual relationship of that detail to the lives of those intersecting on the page. This is where the telling gets interesting. This is where the investigation begins to play itself out.

As the poet said, all the world's a stage.

Little rule: Spell all the words correctly.

Big rule: Pick the right words, and understand their history to take full advantage of their reach.

Little rule: Use colorful language.

Big rule: Metaphor is always more telling than plot.

Little rule: Most people in this life wouldn't know a metaphor if it bit them on the ass.

Big rule: But they'd feel it.

Little rule: Pay attention to chronology—or, more precisely, the causally related chain of events, which may or may not be revealed chronologically.

Big rule: Form is the organic consequence of the relationships amid subject, point of view, and the passage of time.

Little rule: Pay attention to your craft.

Big rule: Pray to God, but always row for shore.

Big rule: Never, never let what anybody says stop you from writing what you believe.

Little rule: Listen closely to what others have to say, especially if they have been kind enough to read your work.

And remember that's what it is, work. Your Life's Work.

If you expect nothing from it, you cannot be disappointed by what it does not bring you. It's a vocation, not a job, and certainly not a career. Remember that little terrier, sitting on your lap while you watch the Oscars, your fist full of popcorn—*nobody reads anyway.*

Remember that golden retriever, bringing to you the blue leash, saying, *Let's go outside and play.*

Fetch, and chase.

Scratch me behind the ear.

Make sure I get my shots.

Don't get mad just because I shed. It's a change in climate, it's not my fault.

Remember to have a little faith. When you die, I believe, God isn't going to ask you what you published. God's going to ask you what you wrote.

It is always okay to question one's faith. It is always, always okay to ask, *Why am I doing this?* "What boots it," John Milton wrote, "to tend the homely slighted Shepherd's trade?"

Milton also wrote, among other things, *Paradise Lost.* He wrote in his Sonnet XIX, "They also serve who only stand and wait."

Milton is what we call a big dog.

Doubt is a storm. We either ride it out, or we change our course. Neither is right or wrong—to stay or go. Twenty years ago, should you have really married X, or Y? This college, or that? A life-changing decision one makes becomes the right decision by the fact of simply having been made. Meanwhile, it is the process of decision-making, the back and forth state of confliction (consider a dog's tail, wagging) that is so impossibly confus-

ing to negotiate. For example, I thought I wanted to be a doctor until I realized I did not like the sight of blood. So I changed my mind. I decided not to become a doctor, and I think my writing life has been informed by that decision—by that willingness to acknowledge my aversion to the sight of blood, especially when it has been spilt upon the floor of, say, violence, or neglect.

Never confuse autobiography with fiction, the impulse to tell your own story with the impulse to tell the story of the world.

After 9/11, like millions all over the world, I was compelled to re-evaluate what I was doing with my life. I used to think I wanted to write something that would last. Now, in the winding middle years of my life, a husband, a father of three, now I understand that nothing lasts. That nobody writes in stone. Everything we love must perish. If it's true for you, it's going to be true for lives you invest upon the page.

This, we call in the trade, an epiphany.

This is what I tell myself *and* my students. Write to understand your place in order to make the world for all of us a better place. Never confuse autobiography with fiction, the impulse to tell your own story with the impulse to tell the story of the world. All great literary art involves at its core a fundamental act of empathy and compassion. Find a subject worthy of your talent. Do not be afraid of silence.

Be bold. Risk it all. Know the rules in order first to learn their purpose, and then to break them, and then to make your own.

When in doubt, give. Always, always give.

And remember, too: You are always free to change your mind.

"In the beginning," wrote Saint John, "was the Word."

Rejoice, therefore, in the kingdom of possibility. Rejoice in the fact of your thumbs. 🍃

T.M. McNally

T. M. McNally is the author of two award-winning collections of short stories, two novels, and most recently the novella *The Goat Bridge*, portions of which received the Faulkner-Wisdom Gold Medal for the Novella. He has received fellowships from the National Endowment for the Arts and the Howard Foundation at Brown University. He teaches writing at Arizona State University.

Eat First

by Joan Silber

My grandfather, who dreaded social occasions, thought that if you were going out to a party, you might as well eat first. If the food was bad, you wouldn't starve, and if the food was good, you wouldn't make a pig of yourself. Though this advice was passed on by my mother as a family joke, I notice I believe in preparing judiciously through nutrition for whatever might happen next. I am one of the few writers who like to chow down before giving a reading. And I always eat before I write.

I write in the afternoon. (Forget morning.) This means that if lunch is over, it's time to write. Naturally, I dawdle over lunch. Sometimes I have three desserts just to stall. In my first college teaching job, a survey by the English department asked people if they used delaying tactics before they wrote, and 100 percent said yes. The researchers concluded that procrastination was part of the process, a happy thought. Certainly some very enjoyable moments of my day are spent procrastinating. While I am having one last cookie, reading one last newspaper article, I am full of hope. Soon I'll be writing superbly, soon, soon.

Extended too long after lunch, this sort of delicious anticipation turns to anxiety, which is when I get to work. This is a more reliable procedure than it sounds.

When I was a younger writer, the hard part for me was showing up. So self-bribery before the task was even begun was quite helpful. By now repetition has taken away certain forms of resistance; I don't feel right if I'm not trying to write at a certain time of day, if I have any choice about it. I'm a slow writer—I revise every sentence as I go, the way you're not supposed to—so my writing demands on myself are in blocks of time rather than in page counts. If I can stay at the desk for a certain number of hours, I feel okay. Usually.

In my twenties and early thirties, I used to work at night. Between ten at night and two in the morning were really good hours, and the phone never rang. I changed to afternoon once I was living with another human being, and though I missed the intensity of those smoke-filled contemplations in the hour of the wolf, I liked the feeling of joining the workaday world. I liked having the writing be a job.

In my twenties and early thirties, I used to work at night. Between ten at night and two in the morning were really good hours, and the phone never rang.

But not too much of a job. I chose it freely and I like to think of it as allied with pleasure—also secrecy and a necessary edge of transgression. So it's probably a good thing that I've managed to shape my schedule so that writing is forever associated with dessert.

I should probably say that I'm not a fat person. Food, since I think about it so much, frequently enters my fiction, though menu items my characters eat with joy—sushi, oysters, purslane salad—aren't necessarily things I like. These preferences are meant to be aspects of character, just as sex in fiction is usually about character. I love to read about food and know more about it than I put into practice; often I have *Gourmet* magazine in front of me while I am chewing on my pre-work tuna-fish sandwich.

I don't get to write every day—I have a real job, after all—but the afternoons I spend at the desk have their own texture and sequence. There's the going over what I wrote before, the Googling for crucial facts, the getting into it, the going off-track, the doubling back. It's not a trance. Toward the end I keep checking the clock, hoping it's near seven, when I can stop to walk the dog, watch the news, and eat dinner. Did someone say dinner? ❦

Joan Silber

Joan Silber is the author of *Ideas of Heaven*, nominated for the National Book Award, and four other works of fiction. Her stories have been published in *The New Yorker*, *Ploughshares*, *The Paris Review*, and other magazines. She's received awards from the Guggenheim Foundation, the National Endowment for the Arts, and the New York Foundation for the Arts. Silber lives in New York City and teaches at Sarah Lawrence College and has taught in the Warren Wilson MFA Program for Writers. She is currently at work on a novel about travel, and is also writing a book on time in fiction for Graywolf's Craft of Fiction series.

Blow It Up

by Stephen Kuusisto

When I was small I could see that the Irish side of my family was colorful and more than a little dangerous. My maternal grandfather, William Marsh, was an early manufacturer of motorcycles and he lived to make enormous amounts of noise and go fast. During World War I he transformed his motorcycle factory in Brockton, Massachusetts, into a munitions plant and sold artillery shells to the U.S. government. On the weekends he would drive into the wilds of New Hampshire and indulge his love of racket by blowing things up with dynamite. By *things* I mean real things: abandoned houses, telephone poles, old machinery and the like ….

Sneaking into an adjacent state and exploding the occasional outhouse won't make you a better writer, but it *is* true that life lived adventurously will yield unexpected joys or exotic failures. My grandfather's diaries are illegible because he lost several fingers while arranging his blasting caps. Nevertheless, if I have a rule of thumb when teaching creative writing or editing the work of my students, it is quite simply: Blow it up.

We are writing in an age of stylish minimalism that in turn has become even more cautious because of computers and word processing. Nowadays, creative writing students are *underwriting* rather than overdoing it. Go to your local university's rare books and manuscripts archive and look at the rough draft of something—*anything*, a typescript by Mark Twain; a hand written draft by Edith Wharton—you will see that there are moments when the writer was going along smoothly according to the basics of the plot when he or she was seized by a larger idea. They knew how to "blow it up" because they weren't writing in the age of instantaneous erasure.

Genre doesn't matter. Blow it *up*. In a story, even the most casual character deserves at least seven words. Nonfiction? Remember what Tom Wolfe called "status-life detail." Show us the gold tooth and the nervous eyes of the pawn broker. What's on the wall behind him? Blow it up. In poetry, whether it's blank verse, a pantoum, or a variant of what used to be called free verse, the image should lead to further disclosure about the mind behind the poem. Let things flow and suggest more creatures of the imagination. Much contemporary poetry ends with the minimal epiphany. Write past that impulse and see if the poem will grow. Blow it up.

My grandfather saw possibilities in abandoned things, and although he lived in an uncultured state, no one ever arrested him. 🦃

We are writing in an age of stylish minimalism that in turn has become even more cautious because of computers and word processing.

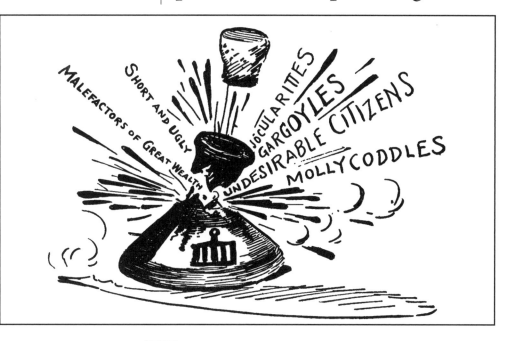

Stephen Kuusisto

Stephen Kuusisto teaches writing at Ohio State University and received his MFA from the University of Iowa. He is the author of *Author of Planet of the Blind: A Memoir* and a poetry collection, *Only Bread, Only Light.* He is the editor of *The Poet's Notebook: Selected Journals of American Poets* and a contributing editor to the *Seneca Review.* Kuusisto's poems and essays have appeared in *The New York Times Magazine, Harper's* and *Poetry,* and he lectures widely on disability and public policy.

A Writing Habit

by Lydia Davis

I suppose the most consistent or comfortable part of my writing process or practice, though it wouldn't suit everyone, is a certain amount of chaos or mess. Involved in this chaos or resulting from it, in a healthy way, seem to be: productivity coming out of patience, or, to put it the other way around, patience first, and at last productivity. ... What is my chaos? I am really talking about beginning and working on more than one thing at a time, so that you have many things in many stages of development, which might bother some people. Having many things in progress takes the pressure off each thing, and also gives it time to ripen on its own, or, since it can't really do that, since that is only a manner of speaking, I mean that you spend time away from it involved with other things, and then come back to it and see it differently, and it appears to have ripened on its own. You are busy working on one thing, but you are not nervous because you have five or six or more other things waiting to be worked on. You have plenty to do, and other things to turn to if this doesn't work out. By patience, I mean you have the patience to return to each thing and reread it until it is really done, which sometimes means waiting for a long time. You may have to wait weeks or even months, if not longer. You are not satisfied with a thing until every part of it is as good as possible, and if it still doesn't seem good enough, after a lot of rereading and reworking, then you are willing to put it away and sit on it as long as necessary, until you really see what it needs or what its true nature is. And in the meantime you don't show it to someone else in hopes that that person will love it more than you do.

I can't exactly command productivity, but it is nice to be productive. It is nice to have so many things in progress that you forget what they're like until you read them again, with great pleasure.

I do recommend this sort of patience. You work on it and then leave it alone and turn to another thing you have begun or nearly finished, and you have fresh energy to work on that, a different kind of energy, even if you were sapped by the first thing. Then sometimes you even turn to a third piece of work. And with luck you'll get a good brand-new idea for a new piece while you're already at work on something. And part of the mess in which you work is that you are willing to turn aside to follow out the good idea, if you dare to leave the other thing you're working on. If you keep starting and working on new things, happily, while still paying attention to the things under way, you may become quite productive. I can't exactly command productivity, but it is nice to be productive. It is nice to have so many things in progress that you forget what they're like until you read them again, with great pleasure. It's nice to have a short memory, to this extent, that you can forget a thing, or at least its nicer nuances, till you read it again. With luck, you can also see immediately what isn't so good, and out that goes. So you have this amount of chaos and then from it coming a piece of work that is not messy, but worked on with great care and attention, with every part of it considered; and behind, in the distance, you have the other pieces of work at their various stages. It should all feel quite friendly. That is the ideal, or I should say that is what is comfortable for me anyway.

Now wait: I have just gotten another idea for an answer to this question of what I care about in writing, maybe an even better idea (while working on the first), but it's probably too late. I'll tack it on anyway: Look up words in the dictionary. Look up etymologies. And one more thing: Care about every comma and semicolon. That's what I guess I meant earlier by care and attention to every part: care and attention to the meaning of every word and the placement of every comma. A comma or lack of it can be so eloquent. ❦

Lydia Davis

Lydia Davis, a 2003 MacArthur Fellow, is the author most recently of the story collection *Samuel Johnson Is Indignant* and the new translation of Proust's *Swann's Way*. She has received grants from Ingram-Merrill Foundation for her fiction and the National Endowment for the Arts for translation; her fiction has won the Pushcart Prize and the PEN Syndicated Fiction Contest. She currently resides in upstate New York where she teaches writing at Bard College.

Upholsterer's Block

by Dan Barden

I became a real writer after college, in the wreckage of my twenties, and I felt like I was inventing it from the air.

How often does someone ask what kind of underwear you prefer or whether you shave in the shower or before you get into the shower or after you get out of the shower?

I love it in *GQ* or *Esquire* or *O* magazines when they tell you the correct way to tie a Windsor knot or what the best flashlight batteries are or what kind of wristwatch the actor Trevor Howard was wearing when Nazi fighter pilots shot down his plane thinking he was Winston Churchill.

I'm old enough to remember typewriters, and even then I wanted my final draft to be pristine. And I mean *pristine*. These days, manuscript prep is easy, but there's still a masochistic part of myself that's nostalgic for that moment when I had to ask myself if cutting that one word on the second page should mean that I retype the whole twelve-page story. The answer was always yes, and I am freakishly proud of that.

Even with my PowerBook G4, I am insistent that no right margin should ever be too jagged. If I write a paragraph that leaves big valleys in the right margin, I will revise those big valleys away.

Another thing: I'm always typing up someone else's work while I'm writing my own. That is, if I'm writing an essay, I like to be typing up someone else's essay. If I'm writing a novel, I like to be typing up someone else's novel. I try to get the best sample I can find, but it's not strictly about modeling great writing. Sometimes when I sit down to my computer I am so damn scared that it's reassuring to know that I can at least *type* good sentences. It calms me to feel the language—our language—move through my fingers.

I never thought that I could do this, and, even now, I doubt that I'll be able to do it again. I became a real writer after college, in the wreckage of my twenties, and I felt like I was inventing it from the air. Although I knew plenty of writers and I'd read all the *Paris Review* interviews, a vocation seemed distant from me as I sat in my apartment in Laguna Beach and wondered if maybe God really wanted me to be a real-estate broker. I wonder if plumbers and carpenters need to feel *entitled* to be plumbers and carpenters. Does an upholsterer ever feel upholsterer's block?

I began to grasp certain principles that got me to work. I learned none of this in graduate school, although I will be eternally grateful for that opportunity. My friend Michael Stephens, for example, told me that he could finish a novel on a half-hour a day, but he could *not* finish a novel on six hours every Saturday. I wrote a fan letter to Walker Percy shortly before he died, and he responded within the week. He shared with me the prayer he said before work each day: "I am starting from nothing. Help me."

I found three principles that are the bedrock of my writing discipline.

1. Writing can be defined as "not doing anything else besides writing." I don't write: I provide the space for writing to happen.

2. Regularity is much more important than duration.

3. If I knew what I wanted to say, I wouldn't have to write, I could just say it. ❧

Dan Barden

Dan Barden is the author of *John Wayne: A Novel*. He received his MFA from Columbia University and currently teaches writing at Butler University in Indianapolis. His work has appeared in *GQ*, *Details*, and other publications.

Writing That Sings

by Jiro Adachi

Hear me now or regret it later: *Everything you write should be read aloud.* Once all the content items are in place, this is the ultimate test for any written piece. Yes, you've heard this before in composition classes, fiction-writing classes, poetry classes. So what? How will it improve your writing? It won't. By itself, reading your work aloud will not improve an iota of your writing. But, reading aloud is a diagnostic test that informs you if your piece is actually finished or not and where to begin revising.

Case in point: I have a friend, a writer of lyrical, haunting short fiction, a graduate of a top MFA writing program, a published writer, a guest of many a sweet writer's colony—in a word, accomplished. A few years back she gave me a draft of a story that she had been working on for months, writing and revising, writing and revising, as if possessed. When she gave it to me, the first thing I did, of course, was put it to the test: I read it aloud. It was as though I was trying to tell a story with a mouthful of toothpicks.

"Did you read this aloud?" I asked her on the phone.

Silence. In her wordlessness, though, I could hear her embarrassment; she had heard me rant many a time about how important it is for writers to read their work

aloud and how pissed off I get when a writer clearly has not. I am a demanding reader. I want music in the prose I read.

Do not neglect your sense of hearing in the process of writing and reading. As a longtime teacher of English as a foreign language, I can tell you on good authority that you have been listening to the English language at least five or six years longer than you have been writing and reading. And, most probably, your ears also had eighteen or more years of

familiarity with the language before you began to read or write with a writer's sensibilities. For these reasons, your ears know when things sound okay, good, beautiful, strange, awkward, or just plain bad, before your eye can pick up on such things. By reading your work aloud, you are using a most valuable editing sense: your hearing.

Get used to reading your work aloud, but also have someone read your work to you. As you listen, ask yourself: Has it ripened? Is the voice fully formed? Is it what you envisioned or hoped for when it first began to crystallize in your perfect imagination? The answers will give you invaluable information for your revisions. By

Your written voice should burn with the fire of fervent prayer, soothe like a friend's voice during a late-night phone call, allure like a lover's whisper.

engaging more of your senses, you are enabling your brain to work harder at crafting an authentic written voice.

Regardless of the form of your work—an essay, a story, a poem, a feature—*someone* needs to communicate the words. Whether it is you, a persona in the guise of a first-person character, an omniscient narrator—for my taste, there must be an accessible *human voice* connected to the word choice, sentence structure, punctuation, rhythm; otherwise the piece is unsuccessful.

And this is the key word: *accessible*. I want my writing to slip seamlessly into a reader's consciousness so that he or she is not even aware of reading.

Your written voice should burn with the fire of fervent prayer, soothe like a friend's voice during a late-night phone call, allure like a lover's whisper. You must, through your accessible, infinitely read-aloudable voice, make your audience into an insatiable reader of your words. If this is not the effect that you feel when you read your own writing aloud, then go back to work and figure out which sentences to torque, which words to cut or to add, when to use a semicolon or a dash. Do whatever you need to do—work ceaselessly and steadily—until you can sit back and breathe a sigh of utter relief that you have, at last, made your writing sing. 🐛

Jiro Adachi

Jiro Adachi is the author of *The Island of Bicycle Dancers*, a novel published by St. Martin's in 2004. To create the novel's portrait of bicycle messengers and immigrants in New York City, Adachi used his experiences as a bicycle messenger and as a teacher of English as a Second Language. He is a member of the faculty at The New School and has taught writing and English as a Second Language at Colorado State University, Hunter College, and Stern College for Women. He earned his MFA in fiction at Colorado State University.

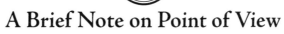

A Brief Note on Point of View

by Marjorie Sandor

Eudora Welty once wrote that "place is one of the lesser angels that watch over the racing hand of fiction" only to lay out, in a richly textured essay, just how central place is to the life of a story. In that same spirit, I'd like to humbly call attention to another lesser angel of fiction: the one sometimes called *perspective*, and sometimes *point of view*, the one that is also so inextricably bound up with voice. Over several years of teaching, I've been most puzzled by my students' shyness when it comes to discussing point of view. Many—both undergraduate and graduate—are visibly uncomfortable with it, and chafe at the notion that there might be rules. But establishing a story's perspective—the time, place, and psychological distance (or intimacy) of the telling and the teller *to* the characters—is central to the power of a story to hold us. When point of view is working at its best, aptly chosen and bravely adhered to, it forms in itself a sense of place, or rootedness, from which the story can deepen or range out with inexhaustible strength and elasticity, making the reader feel, at some level, aware of a pattern, a structural sureness: even if the author chooses to play with, deflate, and undermine that pattern. There is, in any case, a kind of pleasure in feeling the deliberate choice and the wholeness of seduction that comes with it.

A command of point of view changes the writing process itself. For unless you, as the story's writer, have a strong sense of where your narrator is rooted—in place, time, and most crucially, in emotional relation to the story's characters—you will labor on a constantly shifting plane, one that doesn't really allow you to plunge with maximum depth into the consciousness of one character, or move with plausible flexibility and grace among many.

When point of view is working at its best ... it forms in itself a sense of place, or rootedness, from which the story can deepen or range out with inexhaustible strength and elasticity.

What I see, with some frequency, are violations of point of view that not only confuse the reader on the level of plausibility, but which—and this is really the greater problem—prevent the writer from richly imagining the consciousness—and the secret trouble—of a given character or characters.

Let's say that you've decided to tell a story from one character's viewpoint—or even from several characters' viewpoints, but each from his or her own consciousness, in alternating sections. My rule of thumb for these limited-third-person forays is that you should never turn the camera around on the character and suddenly announce, for instance, "she tossed her shoulder-length brown hair and squinted her blue eyes." This is a fairly primitive example, but it amounts to an attempt, on the author's part, to sneak a picture of the character to the readers in a way that the character herself would not—a picture that, in fact, tells us nothing of her character. If the writer really cares about those blue eyes and that brown hair, she must find a way to reveal it from inside the character's thinking process: "Her mother always said she had the nicest brown hair, but Cammie herself hated it—Jake had once called it mousy, and though he'd apologized right away, it was too late. She knew." This of course is long-winded, but demonstrates a point about point of view: What gets reported *has to matter* to the character. Cammie's own thoughts on her personal appearance might begin to shed light on her insecure interior, the constant flailing between her mother's opinion and her boyfriend Jake's. Maybe they will lead her, in an act of shaky defiance, to shave her head. And what would be the consequence of that? Enough. Just remember that strict reportage from the interior of a character isn't really possible. It will always be inflected by desire, worry, fear. Then the story can begin.

A note about the other end of the point-of-view spectrum, omniscience: Usually, experiments in omniscience fail utterly, and my only advice—to myself and my students—is to read great books and stories that employ some form of omniscience, then study them hard. One of the strangest and most exhilarating moments of my own reading life was when I realized how many apparently third-person-omniscient voices are in fact highly voiced and personal, creating the sense of an *I* or *we* storyteller firmly rooted in a historical moment, who takes us along on his or her investigations of times long past (or otherwise mysterious). José Saramago's *Baltasar and Blimunda*, André Schwarz-Bart's *The Last of the Just*, Gabriel García Márquez's *One Hundred Years of Solitude*, and the slim but stunning *On the Black Hill* by Bruce Chatwin: Look at them closely—and others you admire—and feel the lively, even colloquial, presence of the storyteller, the literal and spiritual and in fact highly motivated *spot* from which a narrator—living, breathing, and full of commentary—ranges forth into many viewpoints, always giving the reader little guideposts or bridges along the way—some of them very subtle, but there,

nonetheless—to indicate the descent into an imagined moment, or the source of a particular bit of knowledge, so that we are dropped down by degrees, as if by rope into an unknown cave, then belayed back again, by the same hand.

In the end, of course, the writer who wants to range out into a broad and varied tapestry of figures must read—and *listen* to—the masters of that tradition, and study them hard. As must the one who wants only to go down into the strange tunnels and caverns of one mind, in one place and time. ❧

Marjorie Sandor

Marjorie Sandor is the author of three books—*A Night of Music; Portrait of My Mother, Who Posed Nude in Wartime*; and *The Night Gardener*—all of which include shocking violations of the "rule of thumb" she discusses in her essay, and all of which were written while she held the point-of-view whip over the heads of innocent and brave young writers from Boston to Florida to Oregon.

Prescriptions/Proscriptions

by Michael Martone

Rrrrrrring! the alarm clock went off." Never begin a story this way.

No cats. No tea. No dreams.

When told to cut, expand. When told to develop, cut.

Show *and* tell.

Always use odd numbers. They seem more real.

Repeat. Repeat. Repeat. Repeat. Repeat.

If you like something a lot, use it again.

Never use *Does it work?* or *Does it flow?* when speaking of fiction.

The Theory of Neat Stuff: Not everything has to contribute. Some things are just neat.

Digress aggressively. Break the tyranny of the time line.

Did I tell you to repeat?

You can start a story with a coincidence, but you cannot end with one.

Don't do anything half-assed.

Lose the mirrors, the photographs, and the card-playing unless it is euchre.

You can never have too much peripheral detail or too little on the color of a character's eyes.

A story is always a controlled crash.

Not the line but the blot. 🌿

The Thumb's the Thing

by Tim Parrish

Be ready to sacrifice your thumb for the draft. I don't mean completely, as in to lop it off van Gogh style. Here are a couple of anecdotes.

Having grown up with a good work ethic and having my share of typical writerly neuroses about regimentation and preparation, I treated sitting down to write as a chore. I treated even first drafts, which I consider the only real fun, this way. So, I'd try and gauge my coffee intake, create something of a plan about starting point and a rough idea of where I would try to go, pace for a while, fret, then sit down as if I were entering a cubicle at the office. And this approach worked pretty well for me for a good while. Often still does.

Then, for two years, I wrote and rewrote a draft of a novel. The majority of this novel was set in the fictional equivalent of the chemi-cal plant where my dad had worked for thirty-four years, my uncle for more than twenty, and I for three weeks that seemed like three years. Work there had been hard and often dangerous for my dad and my uncle, and I wanted to honor their work in my own work habits. Feeling good, I sent the draft off to my agent and to my mentor, Ted Solotaroff. Both said start over. The experience was like a car engine dropping on me. Plus, this news came to me around Thanksgiving, the time of year daylight is dying in Connecticut, and that coincidence didn't help me recharge any. Nonetheless, I tried to shake off the disappointment, retool, and get back to work.

However, every time I sat down at my computer, I froze, as if all the judgment and setback of the unsuccessful draft were being beamed at me from the screen. The keys were sludgy. The charac-

The freedom I felt writing longhand was immediate. My sentences took on different cadences, and I embraced a freeing messiness offered up by scribbling in the margins, drawing arrows, and writing on the backs of pages.

ters I managed to type were dim-witted. Everything was stale. I postponed the actual torture of writing and began to rethink the novel.

By late spring, the sun had come back and the thaw was complete, but I still didn't want to sit in the chair and look at the evil eye. So I picked up a pen and pad and took to the yard, the wind still nippy enough to demand fingerless gloves. The freedom I felt writing longhand was immediate. My sentences took on different cadences, and I embraced a freeing messiness offered up by scribbling in the margins, drawing arrows, and writing on the backs of pages. Not that the work was nec-essarily better, but there was sustenance and even joy in it. I wrote and wrote, sometimes going back to the computer, but mostly staying with the pen. But I had a tendency to bear down too hard on my pen, and by the end of summer, the tendonitis in my thumb burned so intensely that I could barely hold a pen, barely play basketball, had to wear a brace and change the mechanics of writing to something resembling the way I've seen pharaohs in movies hold styluses. That said, the injury was worth it to have gotten back to writing, to have broken some old stiffness in my style and pro-cess and to have tapped into a new creative vein.

I'm not suggesting taking up the pen and dropping the computer for all your first drafts. Rather, I'm saying that my rule of thumb is: When the process or creativity seems stale, shift the draft process. There are books that talk about ways to do this, but I'm pretty conservative in what I'll do and so scoff at something even as innocuous as lighting candles and writing in a dark room. I will admit, though, that once when I felt my style was too conservative for a particular story, I went for a run (a run!, with no basketball goal up ahead and no one chasing me), came home, turned on the computer, stood with my back to it, propped the keyboard on my sweaty knee and with one finger typed an entire draft. I had hoped to trick my brain out of its rut, to subvert my typical rhythms, imagery, sentence length, and voice, and I did (along with subverting grammar and punctuation).

Now, I often write in places and under circumstances that I once would not have imagined. Not only with the time-honored pen and paper in a diner (which at one point I would have found too unworklike), but in front of the television (the drone distracting the internal judge) and in the car at stoplights (okay, and sometimes while moving, but carefully). I'm sure this seems familiar to some of you, but for me it was a revelation to be able to change the process and set my imagination free from the punch clock. 🐛

Tim Parrish

Tim Parrish teaches fiction writing at Southern Connecticut State University and is author of the story collection *Red Stick Men*. He was a 2001 Walter E. Dakin Fellow at the Sewanee Writers' Conference and a 2001 Connecticut Arts Fellow.

Revising Revision

by Valerie Miner

I enjoy revision. I hate revision. More important, I *believe* in rewriting my fiction as a mode of discovery and clarification. As artists mature, we perceive shades and subtleties of expression. We adapt in some ways to a common language. We use this language to convey our needs and feelings and ideas. Sometimes we have to rephrase to be understood. Growth is evolution is revision. As Vincent van Gogh wrote to his brother Theo from Arles in September, 1888,

> And to get at that character, the fundamental truth of it: That's three times now that I've painted the same spot. ... But this corner of the garden is a good example of what I was telling you, that to get at the real character of things here, you must look at them and paint them for a long time.

The act of writing is not all climax. Attention to process brings invigoration, meditation, the sweet rhythm of one word breathing against another. Poet Richard Hugo said, "Truth must conform to music." But impatience for crescendo is a characteristic of many good writers. And impatience for gratification is perhaps most raw and honest in young or emerging writers.

In this package-and-market world, it's easy to lose touch with the satisfactions of doing the work itself. Many of us don't give ourselves enough time for our writing. Then, because time is short, we procrastinate (in anger or panic) and waste the hours we have. There's nothing wrong with a deadline, but those of us who depend on deadline motivation might do well to cast a generous fence around our garden. Next time we start a story or a chapter, we might grant

We would do well to attend more closely to the distinctions between view and see, between express and explore, tell and relate as well as to the interrelationship among being and becoming and letting go.

ourselves a week or two longer than what seems necessary. People talk about books and paintings and performances but more rarely about word-play or sketching or instrument-tuning or color-mixing.

Storytelling provides a rare assignment in speedy culture: to concentrate, to pay attention. Literature does not happen in a rush. We might be more willing to delete (or save for another occasion) the brilliant phrase if we privately allowed ourselves the pleasures of phrase-making and word-pruning. We *are* part of our *own* audiences. An important part. We would do well to attend more closely to the distinctions between *view* and *see*, between *express* and *explore*, *tell* and *relate* as well as to the interrelationship among *being* and *becoming* and *letting go*. Only if we have fairly finished a fiction—a piece we have witnessed come to full life—will we be able to start afresh.

Here's how I do it. I drink gallons of water. And too much coffee. My first impulse to write usually comes from character, place, or moral/philosophical quandary. After I know something about the nature of a story, I do research. Then writing. Then editing. Then more research. More rewriting. I ask for feedback. Then it's more research. And further rewriting.

The first draft is written by hand with black ink on lined paper. Typing doesn't work for me on the first draft. I have to move at least as slowly as handwriting. And by skipping every other line, I allow for impulsive changes as well as for a certain kind of airiness to and detachment from the text. Day by day I fill the pale yellow pages. Sometimes stopping because it's too intense. Sometimes obsessed and unwilling to rest. Then I put it out of my consciousness for a time—write something else. Concentrate on my day job. Do the laundry.

Next, I read through the book, making changes in theme, content and language. On the tablet. Then I type the entire draft—all the chapters—into the computer. It helps me to repeat every word, every breath of a story, to reacquaint myself with the small narrative details and to attend to the music of the language.

Once I have a good draft, I print a hard copy for selected readers and take another artistic pause. I look for candid, critical readers who are willing to enter into this project's imaginative world. Each of my books is read in draft by about twenty generous people. I have a few regular reviewers, but every project also requires some specific expertise or sensibility. I asked a lawyer friend to read *A Walking Fire* with close attention to the legal issues. An Asian American friend read *All Good Women*, commenting with particular helpfulness on my portrayal of a Japanese-American family.

Several weeks before readers respond, I read the manuscript aloud to myself. Reading it aloud—like typing it from the handwritten copy—is, partially, a discipline in paying attention. While reading silently, I may gloss over a stylistic awkwardness or a knot in the story line, but my speaking voice focuses my concentration. Besides, I consider narrative an oral tradition and think that a good novel or story moves us with its linguistic rhythms as well as with character and plot.

For me, typical problems include lack of clarity (often when I myself am not sure of a character's motivation), overelaborate metaphor (when I'm trying to accessorize the story), narrative inconsistency (when I'm writing too fast) and excessive explanation (when I lose faith in the reader's intelligence or concentration). Each of us has our individual kinks and equally quirky remedies. Flaubert spent a good deal of his time crushing the proliferating metaphors he called vermin. What works for one author doesn't necessary help another. The trick, I think, is to welcome revision as an opportunity and to be patient. Chekhov advises, "My own experience is that once a story has been written, one has to cross out the beginning and the end. It is there that we authors do most of our lying."

I scribble changes or questions on the hard copy. I do more research. There's always further reading or interviewing or meditating. By working in layers like this, I avoid getting paralyzed by too much background material. I learn that some early questions are inconsequential and I face new problems that now need solving. At this stage—in the middle of construction—I also consider possible structural changes. Of course, I began the book with some sense of its form. But I've never been able to divine the ideal location for the story to unfold before I've written it. I'm more a renovator than an architect, preferring to imagine and tinker from within the house that the story itself has created.

When readers return the manuscript, I take account of general comments, then go through the book page by page in a conversational way, noticing that Eve has said this and Herb has said that. Sometimes readers will like a character or phrase. Sometimes they take opposite positions. Sometimes I make a change. Sometimes not. I am free to disregard advice. But if all readers are baffled by something, I usually expand or edit for clarity.

Once my changes are noted on the hard copy, I pull out a fresh disk and retype the entire book into the computer. This whole process—of writing and waiting and requesting feedback and rewriting and editing and retyping—repeats seven to ten times, depending on the book. Of course, with each draft, I also do page-by-page on-screen editing, but the real imaginative process seems to happen when words and phrases and sentences travel back and forth through my bloodstream, into my typing fingers and onto the page. In *Voicing Our Visions*, a different rendition of this rhythmic process was described by sculptor Barbara Hepworth:

> The left hand, the thinking hand, must be relaxed, sensitive. The rhythms of thought pass through the fingers and grip of this hand into the stone. ... It is also a listening hand. It listens for basic weaknesses of flaws in the stone; for the possibility or imminence of fractures.

Revision, as a form of savoring, is its own pleasure, an expression of internal authority. If I rely completely on on-screen editing, I miss repetitions, factual errors, inconsistencies of dates and names. I find simple computer editing makes it easier for me to ignore awkward language. However, it's unbearable to retype a rotten sentence five or six or seven times. Pride licks my laziness there. This process works for me; I need to witness the pulse of the book with my eyes and fingers and gut. Perhaps if writers enjoyed a fuller experience of the private gratifications of art-making we would be less intimidated by the rigors of revision. ❦

A longer version of this essay was published as "To Look Again" in the September 1995 issue of *The Writer's Chronicle*, a publication of the Association of Writers and Writing Programs.

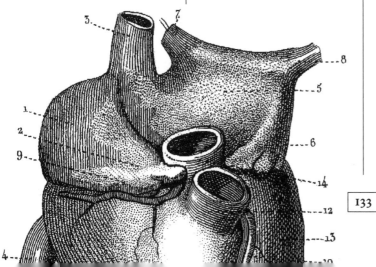

Valerie Miner

A professor of writing at the University of Minnesota, Valerie Miner is the award-winning author of twelve books. Her work has appeared in *The Georgia Review, New Letters, Ploughshares, The Village Voice, Prairie Schooner, The Gettysburg Review, The Women's Review of Books, The Nation* and other journals.

She has won fellowships and awards from the Rockefeller Foundation, the McKnight Foundation, the National Endowment for the Arts, the Jerome Foundation, the Heinz Foundation, and numerous other sources. She also received Fulbright fellowships to Tunisia and India.

Obsessed First-Person Narrators Are the Best First-Person Narrators

by Josh Russell

First-person narrators must be invested in the stories they tell. It's dangerous to use a disinterested or uninvolved first-person narrator, equally unwise to use a first-person narrator whose connection to the story is only slight. While such narrators might seem to bring to fiction objective credibility because they lack motive to tell anything but the truth, their very lack of investment in the stories they narrate negates their emotional attachment. That negation leads to journalistic reports or aimless anecdotes rather than to emotionally authentic narratives. The distance between the story's complexity—be it complex action, emotion, or situation—and the reader needs to be as small as possible, and disinterested or uninvolved narrators add too much distance. If the story isn't in some way about the first-person narrator telling it, then that narrator is in the way of

Self-obsessed narrators are sometimes fascinating, sometimes maddening, sometimes fascinatingly maddening.

the story, adding distance and blocking the view. If you want an objective narrator, use the third person.

The more the first-person narrator is invested in the story she or he tells, the better: Obsessed first-person narrators are the best first-person narrators. Self-obsessed narrators are sometimes fascinating, sometimes maddening, sometimes fascinatingly maddening. The stories they tell are often suspicious, but that suspicion helps good old Coleridgian sus-

pension of disbelief—readers are suspicious of the *narrator*. Narrators obsessed with someone or something other than (or in addition to) themselves also ease that suspension by luring readers into the story: Nothing makes someone or something more attractive or interesting than knowing that someone else thinks the person or thing is attractive or interesting. Finally, obsessed narrators can't help revealing to readers something about themselves based on their obsessions—sex,

power, monkeys—and their seemingly inadvertent disclosures add complexity to a story while narrowing the gap between the reader and the narrative.

Bonus rule: Monkeys! It never hurts to work at least one into a story. 🍎

Josh Russell

Josh Russell is an Illinois native (born in Carbondale, raised in Normal) and teaches writing at Georgia State University. His first novel is *Yellow Jack*. His stories have appeared in *Epoch*, *New Stories from the South*, and elsewhere.

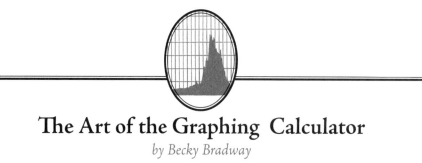

The Art of the Graphing Calculator

by Becky Bradway

Whenever a rule was presented to me, I would resist it. Even if I kept my objections to myself (my usual reaction), I would seethe with inner rage, bubble with resentment, etc., and ultimately subvert whatever it was that I was supposed to be doing. This persistent stubbornness prevents me from relating a helpful or cranky rule of writing. I like to think there are exceptions … those ellipses tossed into inappropriate … places. No rules of grammar or characterization or dialogue patterns for me—at least, none that I'll admit to. What I do have are constants. Let's call them: Requirements of Ambiance.

These well-placed tokens set the ritual stage. Preparation matters. I'm not very spontaneous—and when I am, I usually regret it. I rarely write by inspiration; if I did, I would never write. The arrangement of common things creates a state of readiness, a feel for work imposed around time. Time I might otherwise spend reading a book, watching TV, or cleaning a glass. My things transcend a single place, moving the opportunity into a coffee shop, a train, a bench, a car. My ritual is simple and demanding.

Requirement one: coffee. A potful, if possible, made, if possible, in a medium- to high-quality machine. If no machine is available, but a coffee shop is down the street, then a large whole-milk latte with an extra espresso shot. If stranded (say, on a highway), then any coffee from any rank pot.

The caffeine kick probably has something to do with it. *Everything* to do with it, my daughter would say, accusing me of harboring a dangerous addiction. Physical response hotwired into an electrical system of nerve and muscle resulting in creative output. Except—except—I can do the same with decaf! I really can! It's the act of holding a warm cup (preferably my Intelligentsia Chicago diner mug), hoisting it up, setting it down—having it there—that comforts me. If there's a jitter, hey, all the better.

Requirement two: Pilot Varsity pens, preferably in the colors of (1) purple, (2) pink, (3) turquoise. And if pretty is not available, standard blue or black. No Varsity pen? Then any fine-point felt tip. No felt tip? Well, anything—crayon, pencil stub, Bic Stic.

For me, idea notes and first attempts and editing must be done with a noteworthy (but cheap) pen. My Varsity looks like an old fashioned pen, the kind with a nib—the kind people used with inkpots. Except it has its own ink cartridge, preventing messy globs and spilled ink—and I don't have to feel guilty (or poor) if I lose one. My pen channels long-dead writers who never owned ballpoints but dipped quills into ink and wrote in swirls and slants and dabs. The true ink pen imparts an arty, flowing line. I can pretend to be an artist. A Japanese calligrapher. A signer of the Declaration of Independence. The pen doesn't give me hand cramps. These things matter.

Finally, a beloved pen should never be used to scribble a check to a credit card company, scrawl grocery lists, or take meeting notes. Which leads me to requirement three: the graph pad. Colored,

A beloved pen should never be used to scribble a check to a credit card company, scrawl grocery lists, or take meeting notes.

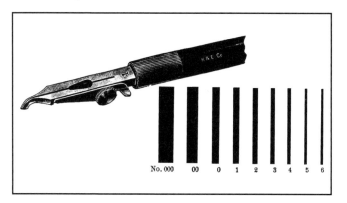

preferably. Conducive for going outside the lines. Since I avoided taking advanced math, graph pads carry no creepy formulaic connotations. For me, they're unique. They seem less demanding of a marginalized left to right. A graph pad permits vertical, sideways, anyways. I rarely put letters in the checkerboards. Yet the squares provide boundaries—less in-timidating and open-ended than white drawing pads or typing paper. The pads aren't meant to be permanent, or even literary, like a fancy leather-bound journal—they accommodate bad attempts, bad moods, wild thoughts. All in all, a graph pad is for working.

The culmination comes in requirement four: restrictive use. The Requirements of Ambiance must only be applied to serious writing. An individualistic pen should never be used when writing a check to a credit card company—that would be demeaning. Likewise, a colored graph pad should be avoided when scrawling grocery lists or classroom notes—otherwise, you'll mix up your rhythmic lyricism with the price of cat food. Coffee, on the other hand, defies restriction; it should be consumed at all times.

My blue graphs and pink pens allow me to separate from those persistent worldly demands: the white white white and black black black of school, of work, of rules. The writing produced is transient, made to evolve or to be discarded. The coffee, too, is momentary—a consoling extension of home, an illusion of high-wire energy. Once the words and pictures come, my talismans are forgotten, and I'm turned loose. And in this place beyond things, beyond judgment, there are no requirements at all. ❧

Becky Bradway

Becky Bradway has published a book of creative nonfiction, *Pink Houses and Family Taverns*, and she is the editor of two anthologies: *Creating Nonfiction* and *In the Middle of the Middle West*. She lives in Bloomington, Illinois, where she works as a freelance writer.

Staunch the Mush

by Debra Spark

"You don't like it when I'm weak," my mother once said to me. She meant when she was sick or crying. I was a teenager at the time. Still, how could this be? Me, a bleeding-heart liberal, irate at someone else's pain? The very Debra sickened by events in Iraq, absorbed with tragedies near and far? The Debra who couldn't watch *Superman* (the version with Christopher Reeve), because it upset her so much when the planet of Krypton blew up and all those people died by plummeting into the black depths of space? (Is that, or is that not, a terrifying way to go?) "You've got," a friend at work once told me, as I was worrying over someone's cancer, "a compassion disorder."

Mom! I think now. *What gives?* And, of course, when my mother accused me, her despair might have been about something like … well, the size of the laundry room. (Sorry, Mom.)

Still, it's true that, as an adult, I don't much like depictions of emotion in fiction. Butterflies in the stomach, hair rising at the back of the neck, a tear rolling down the cheek. So much writing about emotion involves clichés. But even if it didn't, even if you could find endless clever ways to describe dread or satiety or nervousness, you might not want to engage the talent. Leo Tolstoy famously held that art is a means of transferring one man's feelings to another; it's a form of communion. But a portrayal of emotion doesn't necessarily transfer emotion from one man's heart to another. When my son Aidan was a baby, his favorite volume of literature was *Baby Faces*, a book with photographs of babies and a word (on each page) to describe the baby's emotion. I'd turn from page to page, and he'd crack up. "Happy." What a riot. "Sad." Equally amusing. "Angry." More laughter from Aidan. Clearly, feeling was not being transferred from one man's (or baby's) heart to another's.

And why not? Because presenting emotion doesn't necessarily convey emotion. To move your reader to tears—or giggles or outrage or sexual ecstasy or whatever sneaky thing you have in mind—you have to describe what gives rise to emo-

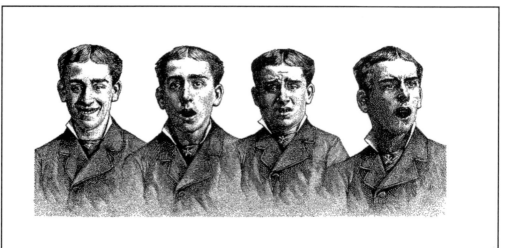

tion. Why is the end of James Joyce's "The Dead" so devastating? Not because Gabriel says, "And then I felt entirely bereft," but because Joyce depicts what happens over the course of an evening, and by the end, the reader knows what Gabriel must feel. So that's my rule (for

So much writing about emotion involves clichés. But even if it didn't, even if you could find endless clever ways to describe dread or satiety or nervousness, you might not want to engage the talent.

myself, for my students): You don't want to present emotion as much as what gives rise to emotion. And a corollary to this rule—a reminder for those who take rules too literally: What gives rise to an emotion might be an event; it might also be a pattern of thinking, a way of processing life that makes—now that I think about it—a closet-size laundry room ample material for a three-act tragedy. 🍎

Debra Spark

Debra Spark is the author of two novels, *Coconuts for the Saint* and *The Ghost of Bridgetown,* and editor of the anthology *Twenty Under Thirty: Best Stories by America's New Young Writers*. Her work has appeared in *Esquire, Ploughshares, Epoch, The New York Times*, and *Food and Wine*, among other places. She has been the recipient of several awards, including a National Endowment for the Arts fellowship, a Pushcart Prize, and the John Zacharis/*Ploughshares* First Book Award. She teaches at Colby College and Warren Wilson College. Her most recent book is *Curious Attractions: Essays on Fiction Writing*.

The Return of the Bread

by Gina Ochsner

It takes courage and a little bit of faith to commit even just one word to the vast blankness of the page. As a chronic worrier in possession of an anxious heart prone to panic, I know this. I'm afraid I'll run out of ideas and that the words will run thin, that I'll wake up one morning to discover the well ran dry in the middle of the night. To combat that fear I force myself to confront it directly—in writing. I write: *I am afraid that I have no ideas left and that no new ones are lurking on the horizon. I am afraid that my fourth grade teacher, Mrs. Wrenk, is right: I am completely unoriginal and I have horrid penmanship.* I start writing my familiar, attendant fears. And then something strange and wonderful happens. Eventually the words *do* fail. The words about how afraid I am and worried and so on *do* dry up and a new word

arrives, an unexpected but most welcome guest. I write it down and then the next word, too. It's a double-dog dare. I'm trusting that the words will arrive, though sometimes it is just one word, one image, one whatever at a time. In the meantime, it's my job to remain awake, alert and faithful to the act. Eventually enough words congregate, shake hands, link arms, and begin their wild waltzing, which I earnestly hope bears fruitful associations, provoking the congregation and collision of yet more words. These I write on little slips of paper, Post-it notes more often than not because they fit in my pocket and I can carry them anywhere. After several days (weeks? months?) of scribbling phrases, a word, an image, a sentence, a single line of dialogue, I'll lay all those little notes on the kitchen table and I'll start shuffling them around, as if they are a shifting mosaic. I'm playing bingo with these little squares and I'm looking for a continuous line in any direction—sideways, backward, forward. I allow myself extra free spaces if I see gaps between phrases. Pretty soon I have what looks like the start of a story. Or perhaps I'm looking at an ending. Or maybe I'm staring at the guts of the slippery middle. It doesn't matter what it is I'm seeing at this point, because what I have and don't have will sort itself out later. I'm combing out the coat of a wet dog, one image, one phrase, one sentence at a time, working the words in any direction they will allow.

And because faith is imagination at its most rigorous and because imagination is an act, I know I must do something with this story. First I'll show it to someone I trust and ask them to read it with a kind heart and a cold eye. After that, it's time to let that story go. I have a yellowed grocery store receipt taped to the side of my computer. It's been there for about eight years and it reads: "Cast your bread upon the waters, for after many days you will find it again." That comes from Ecclesiastes, and I live by this principle. When it looks like—at last—something solid has emerged, a story of substance that I don't think I'll regret having written ten years from now, I let it go. I cast the work out on the water and wait for

I have a yellowed grocery store receipt taped to the side of my computer. It's been there for about eight years and it reads: "Cast your bread upon the waters, for after many days you will find it again."

it to return, trusting that there will be times when the return heralds good news. And the feeling is one of marvelous release—I've fretted and sweated over this story, done all I can do, now it's time to leave that story in somebody else's hands—just where I want it to be. ❦

Gina Ochsner

Gina Ochsner is the author of two short story collections, *People I Wanted to Be* and *The Necessary Grace to Fall*. Her work has been featured in *The New Yorker* and *The Best American Nonrequired Reading*, among many other publications. She has won more than twenty awards for her writing, including the Flannery O'Connor Award for Short Fiction, the Oregon Book Award, and the Pacific Northwest Booksellers Association Book Award.

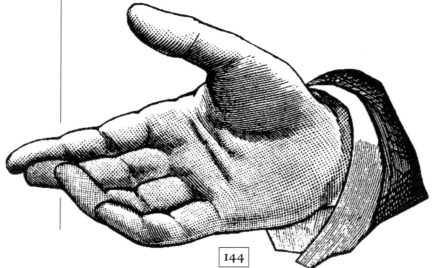

Dress for Success

by Bret Lott

There are plenty of self-inflicted rules I have to observe in order to write: Get a cup of coffee, pray, listen to the same CD the entire time I'm writing a novel—I listened to Charlie Haden and Pat Metheny's *Beyond the Missouri Sky* at least two thousand times while writing the last one—but perhaps the rule I most devoutly abide by is to write in my pajamas.

They're not Dagwood pajamas, no matched set of pants and button-up shirt. Only a T-shirt and shorts. For a couple of months in the winter I'll wear those green and blue plaid flannel pajama pants I got from Old Navy for Christmas one year. No matter the season, I wear a pair of thick socks and these leather house shoes I get at Rack Room for fifteen dollars—I have two pair, in case the first set gets lost or stolen. And there's the blue Eddie Bauer sweatshirt I have to wear, too.

I know these literary vestments stem from *when* I write: I get up around five every morning, and have for as long as I have been writing. Quiet as I can, I put on those socks I've laid out on the floor beside the bed the night before. Then I go to the closet and slip on the house shoes and that sweatshirt. Then I go down to the kitchen and make a cup of instant coffee—the real stuff doesn't get brewed until 6:30, when the automatic coffee maker goes off, so that it's not overcooked when my wife gets up. Then it's back upstairs to the office and a short time of prayer, then to the computer, that CD (right now it's *The Willies* by Bill Frisell), and the story.

And I begin to write.

And because I have been blessed with the *job* of being a writer, that time during which I'm listening to music and sipping coffee can drag on

into late morning, sometimes even the afternoon, when I will find myself out at the mailbox looking for the day's delivery, or standing in the yard while the dog takes her customary three-times-a-day *toilette*. Of course neighbors see me out there in my pajamas—the house shoes, I think, are the giveaway—and although they wave and make small talk, I'm betting the ones who don't know I'm a writer think I'm either unemployed or doddering. For those who are in on the secret, I'm sure they're excusing my dress as being a part of that whole artist thing.

But it worries me, this wearing of pajamas as long as I'm writing, because the kids have

I wear a pair of thick socks and these leather house shoes I get at Rack Room for fifteen dollars—I have two pair, in case the first set gets lost or stolen.

grown up—both boys are in college now—seeing Dad in his pajamas more hours than in his civvies. I fear, no matter what careers they choose, they will live their days with the sadly unfulfilled dream that they might be able to show up at work in their pajamas. I fear that someday they'll pin on me their dashed hopes of pleading a case wearing house shoes and a sweatshirt, or of being able to stand before a classroom to

preach the finer points of the Marshall Plan wearing only a Lemonheads T-shirt and basketball shorts.

Yet however cavernous the curse I have laid upon my children, it is to the written word I must pledge my sartorial allegiance. As I write this I'm wearing the gray sweatshorts and my black Mammoth Books T-shirt, my green SmartWool socks, while literature beckons, and beckons. ❦

Bret Lott

Bret Lott is the author of eleven books and is the editor of *The Southern Review*. One of his novels, *Jewel*, was an Oprah Book Club pick. His stories and essays have appeared in numerous literary journals and magazines, among them *The Yale Review, The Iowa Review*, the *Chicago Tribune*, and *Story*. He has taught creative writing for twelve years at the College of Charleston, where he is a writer-in-residence and a professor of English.

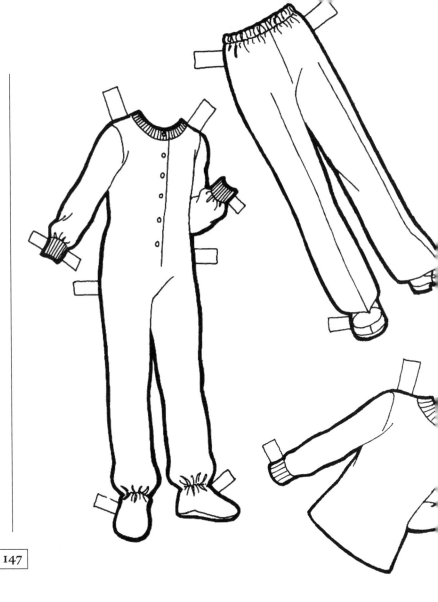

The Busy Attributive: A Case for *Said*

by Steve Almond

The single most annoying, semipro, let-me-show-you-how-clever-I-am-dear-reader literary flourish out there is what I call the *busy attributive*.

It is an ongoing annoyance in my life, and one not limited to actual semipros. No, I'm sorry to report that some of my very favorite writers have been guilty of laying a BA from time to time.

What the hell am I talking about?

Let me start with an example of what I call the *busy attributive flagrante*.

"You look great tonight," cooed the skinny, hairless Dave, while Lucy, who was busy straightening the seam of her stocking, brushed against the man she hoped to seduce, the hirsute and virile Ryan.

The attributive clause (otherwise known as *that thing that comes after the quotation marks*) is not a place where writers should feel free to dump plot information, character sketches, or authorial asides. It has only one basic job: to help convey how a particular piece of dialogue has been spoken.

And even this role, by the way, is limited. Because a good piece of dialogue should—by virtue of word choice, rhythm, and syntax—convey tone.

In other words, if skinny Dave, later on that evening, gets insulted because Ryan is dancing the lambada with Lucy, and says to Ryan, "How dare you, you goddamn cad!" it's really not necessary to use a louder verb, such as *screamed* or *raged* or (God forbid) *caterwauled*. The reader already gets it.

This brings us to a second, lesser crime, the *busy attributive cutesyiana.*

"How did you like that move?" Ryan queried, as he twirled Lucy effortlessly in his strapping arms and wriggled his eyebrows.

Now look: I realize that oftentimes people speak and act simultaneously in real life. And it's awfully tempting to try to reflect this in your prose. But it's also, for the most part, a bush-league move, because readers process sentences discretely. That is: They tend to translate dialogue differently than action. Fusing the two together invites confusion, which is your sworn enemy

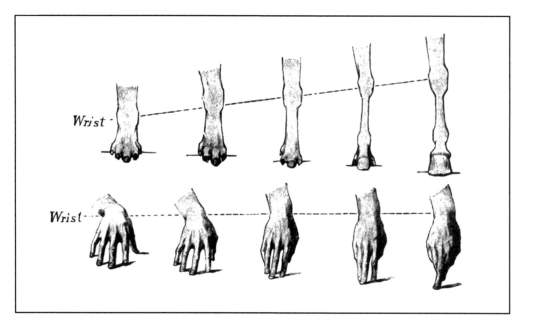

as a writer. It also diminishes the impact of your prose. Consider the above sentence, rewritten:

Ryan twirled Lucy in his arms. "How did you like that move?" He wriggled his eyebrows.

When the snippet of dialogue and the physical gestures are granted their own sentences, they do more work, because the reader is given longer to absorb their import.

Sometimes a writer can go wrong simply by choosing a bogus attributive verb. In fact, there is an entire genus that deserves nothing less than death by blowtorch. I speak, of

course, of the *busy attributive imprecisoids.*

Or actually, I don't speak of them. I *smile* of them. I *shrug* of them. I *scowl* of them. Yes, these are among the *imprecisoids* in common usage.

Here's the problem: you can't *shrug* words. You can't *smile* them. You can't *scowl* them. These are all action verbs that do not, as such, involve the vocal chords. They are gestures. What the writer really means, when she writes:

> "I've seen better dancing in a cripple ward," Dave scowled.

is:

"I've seen better dancing in a cripple ward," Dave said with a scowl.

or, preferably:

Dave scowled. "I've seen better dancing in a cripple ward."

A variation on the *imprecisoid* would be the *lazoid*, which I alluded to above. This would be any of a thousand verbs that attempt to tell the reader how a piece of dialogue is uttered: *begged, declared, mocked, hollered, sneered.*

None of these is technically incorrect. But they still hack me off. Because (again) I want the dialogue itself to convey the effect.

It would be fair to ask, at this point, why writers insist on using busy attributives. It can't just be because they're lazy or evil or trying to piss me off. No, as with almost anything involving writing, the answer is insecurity.

Writers are afraid their stories are boring. Thus, in an effort to keep readers chugging along, they jam as much extraneous info into the attributive as possible. It's like those disclaimers about APR financing at the end of radio commercials.

Writers are also afraid that if they don't use fancy verbs, they will be forced to use *said* over and over again. The reader will then see them as dolts unworthy of sustained attention. I hear this all the time from my undergraduates.

Well, here's a little secret, just between you, me, and the rest of the reading world: *Said* is an invisible word. Readers zip right past it, like the word *I* in a first-person story. If you don't believe me, try reading (or rereading) Raymond Carver's masterpiece, "What We Talk About When We Talk About Love." The story is more than half dialogue. Carver must use one hundred attributive verbs, and all but a handful are—you guessed it—*said*.

There is a final busy attributive I want to note, because it is one even the true pros employ. This is the use of *lie* (as in *deceive*). Here's a passage I came across recently, from the novel *The Male Gaze*, by Lucinda Rosenfeld. Two acquaintances, Phoebe and Susan, meet at a party:

> "Ohmygod, you look so great."
> "Thanks, so do you," [Phoebe] lied. In fact, she'd never seen Susan look worse. Her skin was blotchy.
> It was pretty obvious she'd gained weight.

I don't just find the use of the verb unnecessary; I find it smug. It's as if Rosenfeld doesn't trust us to figure out the truth for ourselves. But this, after all, is one of the great pleasures of reading. The author has put her cleverness before our sense of revelation, and forced us into an unwanted alliance with Phoebe.

It would be fair to ask, at this point, why writers insist on using busy attributives. It can't just be because they're lazy or evil or trying to piss me off. No, as with almost anything involving writing, the answer is insecurity.

I don't mean to single out Rosenfeld, who is a fine writer. In fact, she's in good company. I've seen John Updike, Richard Yates, and F. Scott Fitzgerald do the same thing.

Said is not the only attributive I ever use. I'm happy to deploy an occasional *whisper* or *mutter*. But probably 95 percent of the time I stick with said. Or I ditch the attributive altogether, and allow a gesture to indicate the speaker.

Almond cast a withering gaze upon his audience and cleared his throat.

"Got it?" ❧

Steve Almond

In the eight years since he gave up journalism, Steve Almond has established himself as one of the country's most prolific writers of literary short stories, publishing dozens of them in magazines ranging from *Playboy* and *Ploughshares* to *Zoetrope: All-Story* and *The Georgia Review*. He is the author of two collections of short stories, *The Evil B.B. Chow and Other Stories* and *My Life in Heavy Metal*, as well as the nonfiction book *Candyfreak*. He teaches writing at Boston College.

Contrarian Thumb
by Janet Burroway

The truth does not lie somewhere in between. It lies at both extremes. This, the rule of paradox, seems to me at least as true as the laws of gravity and thermodynamics, more profound than the rules and regulations of an ordered society, and very close to the heart of literature, which is contrarian. People, and therefore characters, are lifelike when contradictory. The metaphor that stretches most says most. Less is more but excess is best.

For something like the same reasons, I eschew writerly advice that begins *must, have to, it is imperative, it is crucial,* and *if you want to sell/publish/be produced.* Particularly I avoid writers who say that you must write in the morning, because people who write best in the morning are subject to a creeping cultural sense of virtue (healthy, wealthy, wise) which leads them to generalize from their own experi-

ence even unto us owls and other nocturnals, marsupials, rodents, ruminants, and burrowers.

Good girls like myself need subversion. Being solemn, I aspire to comedy. Being a novelist, I aspire to the musical. Being organized,

I avoid writers who say that you must write in the morning, because people who write best in the morning are subject to a creeping cultural sense of virtue.

I aspire to luminous chaos. Loving the power of grammar and the fine distinctions of language, I seek the part of my mind I didn't know was there, the part "sheer, no-man-fathomed," "cliffs of fall."

Therefore I live a conventional quotidian life (trying for loyalty, balance, kindliness, not to mention a good pedicure and color-coordinated decor) and when I get to my desk (about noon) try to throw myself off a cliff, which, given all the fences, spikes, guy ropes, customs officers, alarm systems, FBI agents, safety nets, and restraining orders of literature's Homeland Security, is harder than hanging by my thumbs.

The past tense of *lie*, however, is *lay*, and a sonnet has fourteen lines. 🌿

Janet Burroway

Janet Burroway is the author of seven novels, including *Raw Silk*, a finalist for the National Book Award. She also has published poetry, essays, and children's books, and has written numerous plays that have gone on to be produced. Her *Writing Fiction* is the most widely used creative writing text in America, and a new textbook, *Imaginative Writing*, was recently released.

Trimming (Notes to Myself. A To-Do List.)

by Lia Purpura

Do the work of trimming. Pay attention. Watch butchers go at fatty shanks and loins with sharpest knives. Learn about the raggedness of clay to be trimmed from pots and flat forms and see how it falls away. Be in excess more of the time, start there, and then pare. I think I should learn to peel apples more deftly—all around in one long spiral, like old Italian guys, who have time. I think I should learn to quarter and core and set the slices on a white plate to behold the distillation of cream on white. And the shining lamb I keep coming back to, the unresisting, hot, golden fat … cold fat clings terribly, but cooked slowly, for hours, even a spoon can lift it away. And grass: Let it grow wild. Let it tangle. Then harrow with a loud machine, over and over, making paths. Plough down furrows, align crab grass with honest blades of green Kentucky Blue. Following the black wheels, catch fumes. Add from a red gas can when needed.

I should keep a machete near the door. I should switch to the machete more often.

To trim requires abundance. Start with abundance. Clean with a finger the spent

To trim requires abundance. Start with abundance.

coffee grounds in the pot's little chamber: See how much is packed in there. Washing dishes, let the sink fill, fill dangerously high, and when it's stopped and nothing will drain, pick up the mesh drainer and dump the vegetable bits and lumps of soap by hitting it hard against the garbage pail's side. Note the high watermark of grease.

I think I should learn to whittle, and not only to make a thing, but to see how far down I can take it, how far a stick can go in becoming a snake, a needle … what else? What else is in there?

Learning to trim, it would be helpful to learn to pluck a chicken or a pheasant. I suspect it's not a feather-by-feather proposition, but a matter of grabbing a handful and yanking. And making a pile to the side, collecting the feathers to use for … later.

Understand time trims with ease.

Meanwhile, learn to use pinking shears. Practice hems. Mark a line and run the fabric through once and let the same-colored thread bite in. Tie it off. Try the jeans on. There's nothing scraping along the ground anymore or buckling, puckering, wrongly folding. The day itself seems more whole. All of a piece. It's how diminishment makes us free. ❦

Lia Purpura

Lia Purpura's collection of lyrical essays, *Increase*, won the 1999 AWP Award in Creative Nonfiction. A graduate of Oberlin College and the Iowa Writers Workshop, she has published poems, essays, translations, and reviews in many magazines, including *The American Poetry Review*, *The Antioch Review*, *The Iowa Review*, *New Letters*, *Ploughshares* and *Verse*.

Purpura is the recipient of a Millay Colony Fellowship, residencies at The MacDowell Colony and Blue Mountain Center, as well as the Visions International Prize in Translation and the Randall Jarrell Prize. She teaches writing at Loyola College.

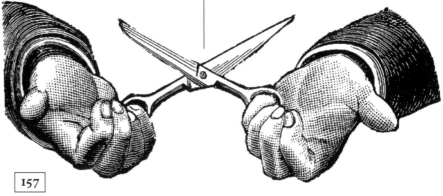

A Sort of Recreation

by Ander Monson

The only thing I rely on in my writing (and which you should rely on in yours, absolutely—unless it doesn't work for you, or if you come up with a better or at least another idea that flies straighter in your eyes or appears otherwise more appealing, because it's more important to be moving, to be writing something that you enjoy, that simply rocks (and that deserves a ! (if not a snatch of air guitar), which otherwise I am sort of stingy with) than to be conforming to my sad pronouncements—though if you'd prefer that I be more absolute about it, hard-nosed, hard-assed, and all, and not leave that escape hatch for you to go through and disregard these words, leave them like an exhaust trail behind you, consumed and rendered into the finest airborne ash that persists in the sky for hours to the pleasure of the thousand eyes below looking up at any time, then I can do

that too (the reasons for this rule—this aside which consists only of asides (of the subversion of rules if you can get your head around it), of modifications, of twists and reversions and slipperiness, of double entendres and stutter steps and hiccups and cul-de-sacs, of doubling back along the sides of the paths we just came tramping down (hussies that we are), of obfuscation and all sorts of syntactical trickery, these methods of literary prestidigitation that we employ to keep ourselves both entertained and on the tightrope facing forward as we make our way nearly to the middle (and this is true, that the exact middle is the saddest moment in any sentence, in any work of any gravity, because it is where gravity—the actual force and not the metaphor for it—begins to exert itself upon the sentence (hence *center of gravity*, the natural mathematical aggregation of all conflicting forces resolved to one theoretical point), where we start to feel the constraints of both received form and the form that we've employed (or, better, created, because that is what we do or want to do, and in wanting, do, at least in theory—never mind the baggage that we drag with us in all our readings and our writings and our experience of genre expectation) in the first half of the piece, in the first half of the summer, where we feel that we are exactly halfway through with something—and even if this feeling's false, that we might know when we are just beginning, or nearly at the end, where we can feel everything coming together, nearly

resonating, closer yet, and the pressure building towards some sort of linguistic breaking point and pause and coming down—that we are equidistant from the end and the beginning, and thus are exerting the exact opposite force on both of these poles, neither approaching nor receding from either one; that regardless of our acceleration, at the exact moment of halfness, we are absolutely still—forget the momentum and the vector we carry with us; right now we

Whatever it is we think we want to say—that is, the main text, the primary thrust—is probably dull beyond comprehension, meaning all has-been, meaning fixed in our intention and thus dead to us (at least for now).

are exactly still, a point with no dimension, no duration), these reasons are (1) because whatever it is we think we want to say—that is, the main text, the primary thrust—is probably

dull beyond comprehension, meaning all has-been, meaning fixed in our intention and thus dead to us (at least for now), meaning time-stop TV has been there, done that, always and forever amen and before, this is to say that the asides, the meanders in the (otherwise apparently straight, when seen from space) river that are all too obvious when viewed with increasing magnification, the tiny inlets and microscopic eddies that make up the current, that these swerves make up the texture of our prose, or of my prose at least (I don't want to suggest that all writing is like mine, except that I obviously do, and am, and thus:), and that this texture is what is most seriously *good* and worth investigating and investing in further and forever, and that all the subterranean and seemingly secondary (or even tertiary) detail—the hatch marks on the wall behind the clock that keeps time over the murder scene—that all these motions away from whatever central thrust we have in mind are yes and bomb and everything, that they deserve all of your attention, that at least they ask you to be open to their implication and exploration if not to the lure of every side road in the city, and (2) that we are (I am) not all that interesting in the end nor finally should we be so invested and headstrong in ourselves to keep out the constant nagging, tugging—all the glorious sloppiness—of the world and the ways it can get underneath our skin) are all tied up in syntax, in case it is not obvious, in the long oration, the stories we keep telling (both to ourselves and to the world at large, if there is indeed a difference) to keep ourselves up on that wire, or a step away from denouement or death, and in the many operations of punctuation (particularly the parenthesis and its companion, as they properly prance around by two, and the glorious sidetrack of the dash) on the vector of the sort of periodic sentence that is such grand fun to explore and tie ourselves in knots (in nooses) with) is detour, is diversion. ❧

Ander Monson

Ander Monson grew up in the Upper Peninsula of Michigan. He lived briefly in Saudi Arabia, Iowa, and in the Deep South, where he received his MFA from the University of Alabama. He is the editor of the magazine DIAGRAM and the New Michigan Press. His stories, essays, and poems have appeared in many literary magazines, including the *North American Review*, *Bellingham Review*, *Ploughshares*, *Boston Review*, and the *Mississippi Review*, among others. He teaches at Grand Valley State University. Tupelo Press recently published his poetry collection, *Vacationland*.

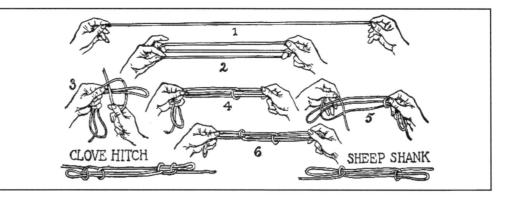

Fifteen Provisional Remainders for the Sake of Clarity

by Joseph Skibell

1. Read the whole thing through at various points without a pen in your hand.

2. Bend your will to the novel's, not the novel's will to your own. Better the piece should succeed on its own terms than fail at some imaginary plan.

3. Discipline leads to inspiration, not inspiration to discipline.

4. Your feelings about the worth of the work will fluctuate wildly during its composition.

5. Try to tell the truth, but from as many points of view as possible.

6. Be open to surprise and divine revelation. In the words of Jackson Browne, "Pay attention to the open sky—you never know what will be coming down."

7. Take a break once in a while, let the whole thing breathe. As the great saint of our generation, Arlo Guthrie, once said, "You can't always do what you're supposed to do."

8. Take infinite care with your prose—then even the white space between the words will resonate with a craftsman's sense of joy.

9. Story above all else: Sacrifice image, theme, meaning, lyricism, intelligent essayistic tangents, all for the sake of a coherent, well-paced tale.

Story above all else: Sacrifice image, theme, meaning, lyricism, intelligent essayistic tangents, all for the sake of a coherent, well-paced tale.

10. Trust in your spouse's opinion. If you're not married, find an honest person who loves you.

11. Accept that the work will at times turn you into a grouchy, unpleasant person. Remember what Joni Mitchell said: "When you dig down deep, you lose good sleep, and it makes you heavy company." Still, as the Beatles promised us, "the deeper you go, the higher you fly."

12. More ideas come from stories than stories from ideas. Anything can occasion a story.

13. Writing well *will* change your life, but not in the ways you expected.

14. On the cold page, the work from your worst day will be only slightly less successful than the work from your best. All drafts are provisional. Learn to work through all your moods.

15. Let there be joy underneath it all, nothing but joy. ❧

Joseph Skibell

Joseph Skibell's novel, *A Blessing on the Moon*, was named one of the year's best by *Publishers Weekly*, *Le Monde* and Amazon.com, and has been translated into half a dozen languages. His short stories and essays have appeared in *Story*, *Tikkun*, *The New York Times*, *Poets & Writers*, and other periodicals. A recipient of a Halls Fellowship, a Michener Fellowship and a National Endowment for the Arts Fellowship, Skibell has taught at the University of Wisconsin, the Humber School for Writers, the Taos Summer Writers' Conference, and Bar-Ilan University. He currently teaches in the creative writing program at Emory University.

Go Where Your Writing Leads You, at Home or Abroad

by Patricia Henley

Walk the streets, eavesdrop at the counter in ma-and-pa doughnut shops, visit the markets, interview hotel maids and refugees and guides who take you to the tops of mountains.

In 1989 I went to Guatemala, seeking stories, but unaware of the fate in store for me: a ten-year literary journey. I met a British doctor there who told me the story of Father Stan Rother, an American priest who was killed in the highlands of Guatemala during the intense political violence of the 1980s. This doctor (his name is lost in the fogs of time) told me that Father Stan's family came to claim his body, and the Mayan people of his village asked if they could cut out his heart and bury it behind the church. They said that his heart belonged in the highlands. When the British doctor told me this story, I was electrified, energized. I knew I had to tell that story.

I set foot on a path that was frightening, exhilarating, difficult, and sorrowful. In the ten years between that conversation with the doctor and holding *Hummingbird House* in my hands, I made five trips to Central America and Mexico, I interviewed refugees, I took surreptitious photographs of military bases, and from each trip I returned to my home in the United States, ready to do the book research. The trips grounded me in the particular, the sights and sounds and smells I could not have invented. I developed an attachment to the Guatemalan people and their land. I spoke with a refugee woman who held her dying child in her arms—there wasn't enough measles vaccine for the children at that camp. I found it necessary to confront such suffering in order to write about it. It seemed the price I had to pay for the privilege of writing about it.

My second novel, *In the River Sweet*, required a trip to Vietnam. I always say that, given the choice, I might have made Thailand or Japan my first Asian destination. But the story line said, *Get thee to Vietnam*. Again, I discovered the details that would have been impossible to glean from all the print material available about Vietnam. Sure, I couldn't have written the book without interviewing people and reading many first-person accounts of the war. But all that reading was no substitute for walking the streets, listening to a boy tap out a tune on a small metal bar announcing that fresh noodles were ready at a food stall, or speaking haltingly with a Buddhist nun in a back-alley Buddhist temple about the time she witnessed a monk setting himself on fire to protest the war. In the former French hill station—Dalat—where my character gives birth, I discovered that there are places in Vietnam where the temperature drops so low at night that you can see your breath. Where the babies wear wool caps in the morning. Where the cabbages grow as big as bowling balls.

Travel stirs the senses and provides particularity. All manner of place indicators will make your job easier. Here's a list of place indicators my students made a few years ago: flora, fauna, landscape, geography, architecture, clothing, food, industry, art, music, population density, body language, weather, climate, vernacular, idioms, work, customs, family names, leisure activities, politics and government, spiritual beliefs, superstitions, folklore, gender roles, and place names. I don't mean to imply that a writer must leave home to write. If you're writing about home, you may need to travel around your town or county and see it anew.

Environmental studies professor David Orr posits that much of what has gone wrong in the world is the result of inadequate or misdirected education that, among other things, deadens the sense of wonder for the created world. He writes in chapter seven of *Eco-*

Travel stirs the senses and provides particularity. All manner of place indicators will make your job easier.

logical Literacy that "unrelieved abstraction inevitably distorts perception." And, "knowledge of a place—where you are and where you come from—is intertwined with knowledge of who you are. Landscape, in other words, shapes mindscape."

Think for a moment about what these statements might mean to a fiction writer. We do not want our perceptions muddied by abstraction, for it is our responsibility, as John Gardner tells us, "to create the vivid and continuous dream," and we do

this through the accretion of those concrete, significant details. In her famous essay on place, Eudora Welty writes:

> Making reality real is art's responsibility. It is a practical assignment, then, a self-assignment: to achieve, by a cultivated sensitivity for observing life, a capacity for receiving its impressions, a lonely, unremitting, unaided, unaidable vision, and transferring this vision without distortion to it onto the pages of a novel.

It's what we writers are about when we take a walk around the block and note the kite abandoned in the vacant lot. And, stopping to see that kite clearly, we take note of the weather—dusty, sunny, or sodden gray—and having done that we may note the girl's ruffled sock in the mud or the boy crying on his back porch. We train ourselves to observe the particular, we fold those particulars into our stories, and it is those particulars that lure the reader seductively into the dream.

It is worth noting that the Welty essay was written in the 1950s and the Gardner ruminations about the art of fiction were published in 1983. What may seem like a long time ago to a young writer. And yet here is a professor of environmental studies—David Orr—who seems to be making some connection for us between then and now. David Orr speaks to me thus: We writers have not been as tainted by abstraction as many folks, and we are the people who might carry that fire—that practice of seeing—to any reader who happens across our work. And when we practice seeing, we are in relationship with what we see. We are shaped by it. Just as our characters are shaped by the landscapes and cityscapes they evolve from. But such seeing is a practice. Just as learning to play the piano is a practice. Or learning to meditate. Or anything worth having that requires self-discipline. It is next to impossible to fill your mind with abstractions and write on Sundays. I believe it's best to be a citizen of the world beyond books and the classroom. Get out there and skydive or spend the summer on an island. Whatever nudges you to wake up and tell the stories only you can tell. ❧

Patricia Henley

Patricia Henley's first novel, *Hummingbird House*, was a finalist for the 1999 National Book Award. Henley has also written two books of poetry, *Learning to Die* and *Back Roads*, and three story collections: *Friday Night at Silver Star*, *The Secret of Cartwheels*, and *Worship of the Common Heart*. Her stories have been published in such magazines as *The Atlantic Monthly*, *Ploughshares*, and *The Missouri Review*, and anthologized in *The Best American Short Stories* and *The Pushcart Prize* anthology. Henley lives in Indiana, where she teaches creative writing at Purdue University.

Junk Your Junk Words

by Wilton Barnhardt

My rule of thumb has to do with all the junk words we use to hedge and hem and soften and blur when we really should be blasting away with clear images and unmistakable language: *a bit, sort of, kind of, virtually, almost* and its partner in crime *almost as if.* I see these in student writing all the time, not to mention in my first drafts. *It was almost as if John wanted to cry.* How does one distinguish between *wanting to cry* and *it being almost as if one wanted to cry?* Junk verbiage proliferates in my classes.

It was sort of gray outside.

The captain thought the sea looked kind of rough this morning.

Her dress was almost as red as a cardinal.

Wallace Stevens had it right when he wrote, "Let be be finale of seem." Give me an is *or a* was *over a* seemed *any day!*

What does *almost* tell me in that sentence? Nothing. Why not leave it at *Her dress was cardinal red?* Because that would be committing oneself, saying it loud and clear, taking on all comers. Many of my grad students think it especially refined writing to see how many of these limp qualifiers can be strung together at once. *It seemed as if it was almost a kind of torture for Billy to sit there.* No, it's a torture for their professor to read a sentence that flaccid.

Which brings us to one of the premier fudge words, the verbal equivalent of camera-lens cheesecloth for aging actresses: *seem.*

Michael seemed to let his father's hand go in the crowd.

Why not *lost his father's hand, squirmed out of his father's grasp?*

The boiler seemed to explode at once.

Why not simply have the boiler explode, disintegrate, obliterate itself?

Father seemed angry when he came home from work.

This is a correct enough usage, but how much stronger it is to write *Father was angry when he came home from work*, and then provide evidence: *slamming the doors, flinging the junk mail with violence into the trashcan, mumbling under his breath.* As writers we're supposed to give the reader distinct and memorable visuals. *Seem* throws all the action back on the narrator: Look what *I* saw, me me me, imagine *my* feelings when … . Curiously, if you take *seem* out of a sentence in favor of a more concrete, accurate verb—even plain ol' *was* and *is*—you usually not only

170

strengthen the visual but also, happily, lose nothing concerning the narrator's perceptions. It's the narrator's point of view, after all, and if he sees things with greater clarity, we can assume as readers that he feels them, too.

So my rule of thumb is use the "Find and Replace" function of your word processor and inspect your fiction for all the lazy uses of *seem*. When real issues of perception are involved, keep it; when it's just fogging up the place where a strong verb is called for, replace it. I don't know what the poem means any more than anyone else, but Wallace Stevens had it right when he wrote, "Let be be finale of seem." Give me an *is* or a *was* over a *seemed* any day!

And don't get me started on the other great junk verb. *Jimmy came home late and managed to fall into bed.* What maneuvers, what complex machinations and managements are required to flop onto a bed? *Managed*, good grief … . 🐝

Wilton Barnhardt

A former reporter for *Sports Illustrated*, Wilton Barnhardt is a veteran of many nationally ranked MFA programs, including the University of California at Irvine and the Warren Wilson MFA Program for Writers. He has written three critically acclaimed novels: *Emma Who Saved My Life*, *Gospel*, and *Show World*. He is currently director of the MFA program at North Carolina State University.

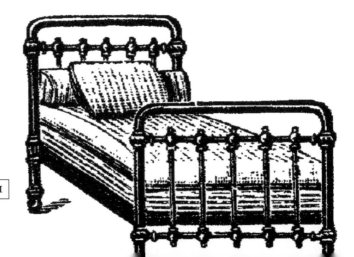

Just Shut Up

by Phyllis Alesia Perry

Once you've answered the storytelling impulse by repeating your plot over and over, your wonderful and complex brain might see no reason to write it down.

Since I started writing fiction, I've begun attending writers' conferences and have had a lot of conversations with people interested in writing. At every conference, I get involved in at least one conversation in which someone is saying something like this: "I have this idea for a book. What happens is … " What follows is a fairly long monologue about her idea, sometimes a very good idea.

I used to listen quite earnestly and quite earnestly offer an opinion as to whether I thought the story line she was spinning would make a good book. What I wouldn't say was that I was skeptical about her even beginning. It didn't matter how good the idea was or whether it was presented to me by an experienced writer or by a hobbyist. The more she got into the plot, the more her eyes glowed with the joy of telling that story, the less I believed it would ever be written.

Sometime not long after I'd endured the agony of writing my first book, I began to understand something that perhaps many established writers already knew, but came as quite a revelation to me. The more I talked about the novel, the less I wanted to write it. But still, it took a few years of listening to fledgling writers talk before I found the courage to tell them what I really thought: that they should stop talking and start writing.

After all, maybe talking about their book plans *did* help them get going. I know a lot of writers work out ideas and plot lines, dialogue and settings in conversation with other people. That's what works for them and there's nothing wrong with doing it that way. There is no wrong way to write, really.

But then people began to ask me if I would read these non-existent manuscripts, after they

had a few chapters, of course, just to see if they were heading in the right direction. I had to say no, and I took the even more shocking step of advising them that they might want to write something before they began looking for editors, agents, and people to reassure them that it was even worth their time. Even though I always gave this advice in as unoffending a tone as

I could, a few *were* offended, some highly so. Wasn't I supposed to be encouraging and kind? Wasn't I supposed to be applauding their ambition and serving as some kind of instant mentor?

Well, maybe. But my first act as a mentor is usually to tell people to shut up. Really.

The desire to tell a good story is beautiful and honest—a way of entering into the warm embrace of community. But once you've answered the storytelling impulse by repeating your plot over and over, your wonderful and complex brain might see no reason to write it down. It's told. It's done.

It may be that my route to fiction writing is to blame for this bluntness. I didn't major in creative writing. I don't have an MFA (I have a BA in journalism from the University of Alabama). I spent sixteen years editing and writing stories for newspapers before my first novel was published. I've never workshopped anything, or sat in cafés debating the intricacies of possible plots.

Writing is a solitary experience for me. I wouldn't want to do it otherwise. In those fresh moments of creation I don't want anyone else around or any other voices in my head except the ones that are compelling me to write. After that first—or often second—draft, I welcome and demand honest, vigorous editing by someone who knows what he or she is doing.

Aspiring writers, this may seem contrary to what you've been told about joining writers' groups or presenting works-in-progress. I'm not saying you shouldn't do those things. But if you're only doing them because you want someone to anoint your effort and tell you everything's looking okay, then stop.

Give yourself permission to write. Be alone. Get quiet. You might as well get it over with at the beginning to see if you can stand it. If the quiet scares you, just live with the fear. If you have been talking a lot about the work you want to do and then going home to stare for hours at your blank computer screen, consider that opening your mouth and yakking has sucked all of the desire right out of your brain. ❧

Phyllis Alesia Perry

Phyllis Alesia Perry is a Pulitzer Prize-winning newspaper editor in Atlanta. Her most recent novel is *A Sunday in June.*

Shape-Shifting

by Philip Graham

The social studies teacher of my sophomore year in high school, Michael T. Hinkemeyer (that middle initial was very important to him), rarely taught us the history he was supposed to. Certainly I can't remember a single detail of whatever we should have studied that year. Instead, Mr. Hinkemeyer (or "The Hink," as some called him behind his back) liked to digress about Hemingway, literature, and the book he himself was working on—a future Great American Novel, he implied, and we believed him. How easily he held us—so young, impressionable, and ready to worship—in his thrall. He was so painfully pale and blond, he looked barely a shade shy of albino, and we believed he was something of a rascal—he flirted shamelessly with the girls in the class. We knew, just knew, that someday he was going to be famous.

He graded our papers as if they were short stories. I especially remember him drumming into us the rule of never repeating a word in the same sentence, which he told us was a signature of Hemingway's style. "What about if you repeat *the* in a sentence?" we'd tease and challenge him, "What about repeating *a?*" He'd shrug off our adolescent wit with a dismissive grin, because his advice was coming from one of the greats—Hemingway had only been dead for about six years, and he cast an enormous shadow.

My secret ambition had long been to become a writer, and so I soon imagined that Hemingway's ghost looked over Mr. Hinkemeyer's shoulder at me as I wrote. Working hard to rid my writing of roughage, I started to sense each sentence possessed a weight, a center of gravity that could be altered with a small deletion here, a minor enhancement there. I began to think seriously about synonyms; I asked my parents for a *Roget's Thesaurus* for Christmas. And what a gift: Thickets of words on each page offered me release from the sin of repetition, but most solutions were never simple when there were all those shades of meaning and implication. I had discovered the muscular, slippery, subtle, and confounding variability of the English language—and something else, too, though I didn't know it at the time: that grappling with a shape-shifting sentence is good practice for life's own shape-shifting mysteries.

Mr. Hinkemeyer didn't return for a second year of teaching. Rumor had it that over the summer he'd been fired for sleeping with one of the girls in the senior class—gossip that, in those pre-feminist days of the mid-1960s, only enhanced the romance of his reputation. Years passed, and I never heard of Michael T. Hinkemeyer again, not after graduating from high school, college, or grad school. Occasionally I wondered, *Whatever happened to the Great American Novel my old high school social studies teacher had been working on?* Meanwhile, my *Roget's Thesaurus* slowly transformed from a book to a companion as I began publishing my own work—prose poems, short stories, a novel.

Then, one morning in 1991 while on vacation with my family, over twenty years after I'd graduated from high school, I turned on the hotel room's TV to check the weather and, while flipping through the channels, saw a familiar face that made me stop. Michael T. Hinkemeyer! He looked as if he hadn't aged a day. He was being interviewed by Oprah, for a show that featured three or four authors of romance fiction. It turned out he'd had a quite prosperous career as the author of such novels as *Flames of Desire* and *Seize the Dawn*, writing under the pseudonym of Vanessa Royall.

176

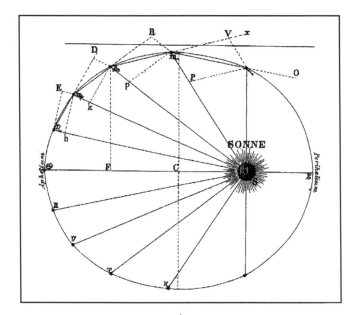

Working hard to rid my writing of roughage, I started to sense each sentence possessed a weight, a center of gravity that could be altered with a small deletion here, a minor enhancement there.

I sat back in my chair, stunned, and watched that once familiar grin from the old days, which hadn't even lost its hint of arrogance—and why should it? He'd pulled off a neat trick, this very male Vanessa Roy-

all who'd written a number of successful bodice rippers, and now he was happy to admit it. The rascal! Not a word about any Great American Novel, of course. Those dreams die hard, and are not to be admitted. The

sight of him brought me back to those days of my first serious struggles with words and their peculiar, individual balances of attraction and repulsion. Here was one of the teachers who'd set me on my first steps towards a life of writing, a man who, I now realized, wrote the sort of books I'd pass by in a supermarket without a second glance. Mentors die hard too, I

supposed, though Michael T. Hinkemeyer had been an unknowing mentor to the secret ambitions of my younger self.

Yet even disillusion alters. A few months ago, over ten years after that shocking sight of my former teacher, an idle, late-night Web search led me to lists of several books—thrillers, mysteries, and crime novels of one sort or another—written under Michael T. Hinkemeyer's own name, as well as a few others under a pseudonym, Jan Lara. Readers' comments on even his romance novels praised the quality of his writing, the deftly handled historical knowledge. I discovered that the French love him and have translated several of his books, and St. Cloud State University has purchased his literary papers, though perhaps mainly because he hails from that region of Minnesota. With just a little Googling, my old social studies teacher had risen in my eyes from a romance novel charlatan to something more like an honorable craftsman.

These days, when I call to mind Michael T. Hinkemeyer, I can see him as a journeyman writer—no Hemingway he—working his sentences as carefully as he can on a deadline, arranging words to rise above whatever genre he was contracted to work in. As for me, my copy of *Roget's Thesaurus* still lies within reach on my desk, the spine now reinforced by tape many times over, and I still worry about repetition in a sentence—barring, of course, deliberate emphasis, or other stylistic quirks that rise moment by moment. But that old writerly rule of thumb has developed a complicated pedigree, because life's lessons shift shape just like sentences. ❦

Philip Graham

Philip Graham is the author of five books, including *Interior Design: Stories* and the novel *How to Read an Unwritten Language*. He teaches writing at the University of Illinois at Urbana-Champaign, is the fiction editor of *Ninth Letter*, and has hitchhiked throughout the United States and Japan.

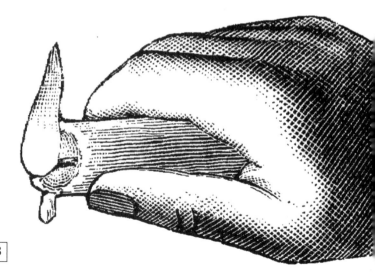

"There's Only One Rule: Never Be Boring" (Henry James)

by David Shields

Because they live in a nation in which it's virtually impossible for a novel to be both interesting and popular enough to create a scandal, American novelists are drawn to the work of *succes de scandale* photographers. Ann Beattie wrote the introduction to Sally Mann's *At Twelve*, then produced a novel, *Picturing Will*, that contains unmistakable parallels to Mann's life and work. Reynolds Price wrote the afterword to Mann's *Immediate Family*, her book of photographs of her three children in various stages of undress and prepubescent sensuality. Jayne Anne Phillips's essay "A Harvest of Light" prefaces Jock Sturges's *The Last Day of Summer*, from which the FBI confiscated some photographs as "child pornography." The epigraph to Kathryn Harrison's novel *Exposure* is Diane Arbus's well-known aphorism—"A photograph is a secret about a secret. The more it tells you, the less you know"—and the book concerns Ann Rogers, the thirty-three-year-old daughter of Edgar Rogers, a retrospective of whose photographs has been scheduled at the Museum of Modern Art. The photographs document Ann, as a child, in poses of "self-mutilation and sexual play."

> *There are works that are merely tricky and then there are works whose structural and stylistic tricks are crucial tools to mine the material.*

Fig.1

Somewhere I had come up with the notion that one's personal life had nothing to do with fiction, when the truth, as everybody knows, is nearly the direct opposite. Moreover, contrary evidence was all around me, though I chose to ignore it, for in fact the fiction both published and unpublished that moved and pleased me then as now was precisely that which had been made luminous, undeniably authentic by having been found and taken up, always at a cost, from deeper, more shared levels of the life we all really live.

—Thomas Pynchon

There isn't any story. It's not the story. It's just this breathtaking world, that's the point. The story's not important; what's important is the way the world looks. That's what makes you feel stuff. That's what puts you there.

—Frederick Barthelme

Beauty will be convulsive or will not be at all.

—André Breton

Have you ever heard a record [Stevie Wonder's *Fingertips—Part 2*] in twenty years that makes you feel so good? I haven't. It's so *real*. When you listen to the record, you can hear a guy in the band yelling, "What key? What key?" He's *lost*. But then he finds the key, and boom. Every time I hear that guy yelling, "What key?" I get excited.

—John Mellencamp

Donald Justice Before a Soft-Drink Vending Machine

He's put his two quarters in the slot
And pressed a button,
Then another
But, nothing.

Again, he presses them,
Muttering, putting some muscle
Behind the heel of his hand,
The ire rising in him, finding

Its level, faltering,
Spent finally in a last muted
Jab and last muted curse, the eyeglasses
Edging further along the bridge of his nose.

He'll not kick the machine
Nor report to the office across campus
For a refund. Upstairs
The students will be reconvening

To their workshop,
Sheaves of sestinas

On their table, their own
And those of past masters before them.

For a moment he stands speechless
Before the looming, mechanical cheat
Full in the glare of its red-blue lights, there
In the otherwise dark passageway.

The two vertical masses
Front each other, so
Then the poet turns and heads off
Toward what he can hope to know.

—Daniel Rifenburgh

The origin of the novel lies in its pretense of actuality. Literary mosaic is a fascinating form, but a difficult one to execute: Momentum derives not from narrative but the subtle, progressive buildup of thematic resonances.

There is formal innovation and then there is formal innovation. There are works that are merely tricky and then there are works whose structural and stylistic tricks are crucial tools to mine the material. Content tests form.

A didactic white arrow is superimposed on the left- and right-hand panels, pointing almost sardonically at the dying man. (These arrows, [the artist Francis] Bacon's favorite distancing device, are sometimes explained as merely formal ways of preventing the reader from reading the image too literally. In reality, they do just the opposite, and insist that one treat the image as hyperexemplary, as though it came from a medical textbook.)

The grief in the painting is intensified by the coolness of its layout and the detachment of its gaze. It has been Bacon's insight that it is precisely such seeming detachment—the rhetoric of the documentary, the film strip, and the medical textbook—that has provided the elegiac language of the last forty years.

`   —Adam Gopnik

After swimming, I'm sitting in the lobby of the recreation center, tying my shoes, and I see someone reading what looks like *Checkpoint*, Nicholson Baker's novel about assassinating Bush. I've just finished reading the book, so I say, "You reading *Checkpoint?* How do you like it?" The reader seems wary and is strikingly reluctant to respond with any specificity to my question until he asks if I'm the writer David Shields. I am, the one, the only. Still, we talk about the book and Baker only circumlocutiously. When I'm ready to go, I well-meaningly but ill-advisedly say, "I'm David Shields, I guess you know that. What's your name?"—which, of course, reanimates the entire spy-versus-spy subtext, so he says, very slowly, "I'm Wes." No last name. End of conversation. A new moment in the republic, so far as I can tell. ❧

David Shields

David Shields is the author of eight books of fiction and nonfiction, including *Black Planet*, a finalist for the National Book Critics Circle Award. He also is the recipient of a Guggenheim fellowship and two National Endowment for the Arts awards in fiction. He teaches at the University of Washington and Warren Wilson College.

Won't, Don't, and Can't

by Cris Mazza

Most of my personal writing rules seem to be in the negative. Tactics to avoid that represent (to me) formula or homogenized story-style or sound like every other story I just saw in a stack of application-writing samples, or just plain immaturity. Of course the danger in admitting to owning them is that as soon as I do, someone will show me a long list of well-known instances of high literary art employing the same methods I've just cited as artfully inferior. Or someone I know and respect or count as a friend will say "whadda you mean it's defective to _____. I _____ all the time!" To that there's always the handy panacea, "I didn't mean *you*." Or "*You* don't do it the way I mean." So, if I offend, consider it already said.

1. I won't start a story or chapter with a character's name. This stems directly from: I will never use the character's first and last name the first time the name is used. The sum is even stronger: I don't start a story or chapter with a character's first and last name.

> Bob Smith unlocked his office door.
> Bob Smith grabbed the stick and shifted his Porsche into second.

I admit to loading the deck with that one. How about:

> Bob Smith was awakened from a dream by his ringing alarm.

Even worse:

> Brrring. Bob Smith jerked awake.

(Although technically it didn't start with his first and last name.)

Starting with some kind of narrative—even if just one sentence—sets the tone, the atmosphere, the situation, the condition for the story and the position the author may want me to be in as I read.

So let's leave the dream and the ringing alarm and the ever-symbolic stick shift out of the equation.

Jennifer Jones looked at her mother and stamped her foot.

It's Starting a Story 101. When you're reading a stack of fellowship or writing-program applications, or contest entries, or even just the regular submissions received by a literary magazine, stories starting with a character's first and last name start to peal repetitively. *I couldn't start any other way, I couldn't start any other way, I couldn't start any other way.* And the occasional: *Of course my character's last name is going to be a crucial piece of language necessary to understanding my story and must be brought to the forefront.* Or not.

2. I won't start a story or chapter with disembodied dialogue. Maybe I'm too poor a reader (remember that stack of applications) but when you throw some dialogue in my face, then some narrative begins, people are introduced, they're doing things—smoking or drinking or running somewhere or peeling potatoes—I'm often not sure who said that first line. It's like hearing a loud statement through a door before you enter a room full of people you don't know.

And again it seems like Starting a Story 101. *Put your reader immediately into the action*, says the textbook. *Okay*, says the author who is consciously following textbook instructions, *I'll put the reader in the middle of a dramatic scene—in the middle of dramatic dialogue in the dramatic scene.*

For me, starting with some kind of narrative—even if just one sentence—sets the tone, the atmosphere, the situation, the condition for the story and the position the author may want me to be in as I read. Opening narrative may convey an ironic slant, the texture of a place, the feel of a span of time, some clue as to which character I need to focus on, whose point of view I'm perceiving, or any other aspect of style that's going to be pertinent to the whole story's effect. Then that early dialogue's impression will not be outside the story; it's going to be more acute, it's going to be more lasting.

These tactics to avoid are trivial. Although I have strictly adhered to them for over twenty-five years and a dozen books, it's easy to say I will never do them without putting a restriction on my range of formal possibilities and continued development as a writer. Now I'm going to mention something potentially more problematic.

3. I have become more and more troubled (perhaps my students would say *aggravated*) by the overuse of first-person point of view. This overuse possibly stems from today's society's thirst for "reality," from confessional talk shows to look-at-me memoirs to reality dramas on network television. To some publishers, first-person narrative just sounds more like a *real* person is telling you his or her *real* story. To some inexperienced authors, writing in first person feels like more deeply accessing a character, because they're accessing themselves. I was once one of these inexperienced writers, at nineteen or twenty,

proclaiming to whomever was unfortunate enough to be my creative-writing professor, "I can't write in anything but first person." Advantageously (for me) some instinct caused me to teach myself to cultivate a voice in something other than first person when, in my first published novel, I created a central character who has no memory of her own past but does have a memory of her lover's past. So, in first-person POV,

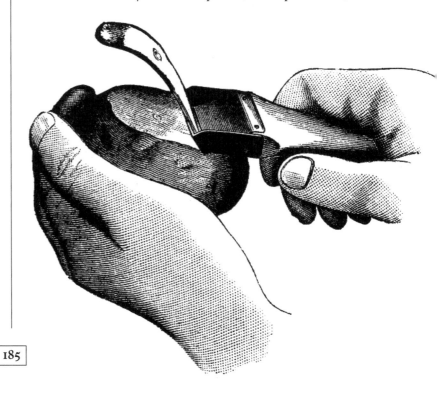

she narrates *his* story—his story before she knew him. The narrative therefore contained no first-person pronouns, generating, of course, a form of third-person limited perspective.

I say it was my first *published* novel because I'd written one earlier that was published after the novel I just discussed. That real first novel was in first-person interior monologue (which, in my mind, I've separated slightly from stream of consciousness, in that I consider interior monologue more accessible than genuine stream of consciousness). Perhaps many writers would like to be able to go back and revise their early books, and I'd be first in line with a copy of that interior-monologue book if the opportunity came about. Not to change the POV from the first person, but to hone the interior monologue, to remove any instances of overnarration and seemingly conscious explanation.

This is where some or most of my discomfort with first-person narrative starts to come into play: I do think first person is grossly overused and has been for at least ten years. But I am probably most bothered by the plethora of first-person present-tense linear narratives used (probably) to sound contemporary or postmodern, or as a flawed attempt at interior monologue.

I am on my way to my lawyer's office and pass a laundromat. I am suddenly filled with thoughts of my mother. I remember how she forced me to go with her when her washing machine broke, and how she tried to have mother-daughter talks while we waited for the first loads to be clean and dry. I regret now how I resisted and acted sullenly. My memories cause me to forget about my looming appointment.

I've stacked this example to more quickly illustrate my point. If I am to read this as interior monologue—a first-person narrative not generated after the events but *during*—I am thrown *out* of the scene, not drawn into it, because this character isn't spontaneously having a memory, she seems to be consciously narrating it to someone (but who?). Instead of immediate perceptions (the sight, sound, or smell of a laundromat) inciting the monologue in her head to wander, she is explaining (to who? to me? to herself?) that her thoughts are wandering. Wouldn't a true interior monologue not need an *I think, I remember, I wonder,* or even *I say?* The thought, the memory, the question, or the spoken words would just suddenly appear in the text. (And consider how many first-person pronouns would be eliminated.)

The steamy air of a laundromat swells out its open door, thick and cottony and clean. A drowsy, cozy, sudden puff of warmth, and yet I pouted and sulked when my mother wanted me to come with her, the few times she ever used a public laundromat.

I can distill my suspicion that first-person narrative—present tense or not—is overused into a rule I've been giving to frustrated students more and more often. The effects first-person narrative have on a piece of fiction are complex. It's not just a convenient process of projecting a story onto paper in a way that feels more like yourself talking. And not just a method to "make the reader feel closer to the character" (how many times have I heard that one, and yet couldn't possibly feel close to the overnarration and overexplanation of the nattering character in question). The fact that a story is being told by one of the characters in the story (even one who has only witnessed the events of the story) has to be part of what that piece of fiction is about. And at this point I admit that they could bring me dozens of published samples that are entirely unaware of this "rule," and I break into my own examples, starting with *Lolita*.

At one time I was fortunate enough to accidentally turn first-person narrative into a camouflaged third, and thus broke out of my self-determined rut, my inability to write in anything but first person. Recently I decided I need to break out of my acute aversion to first person: I'm going to have to remove myself from a rut again, and not just in epistolary moments. Because now it relates to my biggest rule: As soon as you say *I can't* _____, that's when you have to do it.

This rule, however, doesn't apply to *I won't* _____, so I'm still allowing myself to never start with a character's name. ❦

Cris Mazza

A native of Southern California, Cris Mazza is the author of *Indigenous: Growing Up Californian*. She is also the author of *Homeland*, a novel set in San Diego County. Her other books include *Girl Beside Him*, *Dog People*, *How to Leave a Country*, and *Is It Sexual Harassment Yet?* Mazza is a professor of creative writing at the University of Illinois at Chicago.

Ten Signs That You Should Stop Reading Books That Offer Advice on Being a Better Writer

by David Haynes

My children: It's all relative, you make it up as you go along, rules are for fools, honor thy mother and father, do your own thing, write what you know, avoid flashbacks, and make it new.

This one time I had some time to kill, so I was patronizing my local independent bookseller (which, sadly enough, no longer exists), just browsing, no biggie, so I turn the corner past the poetry stacks and I see this section that is just packed with books, and I look up and hanging above all these packed-in books is this big sign that says "Writing," and at first I think to myself, *Hey, isn't everything in this joint writing?*, and then I checked out the titles and I realized that these weren't books, these were the books that told a person how to write all other books in the store; I pulled one down—just reached in there and grabbed one, didn't even check out the title first or anything—and I start paging through the thing and I was all like *Wow!* because, the thing is, it wasn't even really like a regular book at all—it was like a cookbook or something—or like one of those books that tell you how to rewire the plumbing or have a better relationship with your kids and your cat—and I was so amazed, because you see, the thing is: One of the great guilty pleasures in Dave World (which is how I like to refer to my own personal corner of the sky) is browsing in the front of the shopping-mall bookstore through the sorts of books written by TV psychologists, phone psychics, and former child stars that offer advice in list format. How great is it that men and women—many with apparently no more than an eighth-grade education—are able to boil down the wisdom of the universe into concisely worded statements, gathered together under pithy catch phrases ("The Seven No-Nos of Bedroom Etiquette," "Five Signs you Have a Toxic Spouse") and make millions of dollars doing so, and so here I was, in a section made just for people like you and me: And I pull out another title and then another, then another: and guess what I find? No lists. Can you imagine? I think to myself, *What's wrong with writers that they haven't figured out the whole self-help side of helping themselves?* It's like we can write all these other great books that help people attract money and a mate or make a pesto pizza with goat cheese and sun-dried tomatoes, but nowhere on these shelves can I find a "Ten Surefire Ways to Make Your Sentences Sing" and that's when I said to myself, *Dave, This is the job for you: You will be the one to create the first pithy, list-oriented, therapeutic, media-genic, ripe-for-Oprah, best-selling book of writing advice!* and so of course I went home right that minute and began generating ideas for lists and syndromes (because all the best books identify syndromes—which make for easy hooks for Katie when she interviews you on *The Today Show* ["Dave, tell our readers about the Got Ghetto? Syndrome"]) and I had actually spawned ten or a dozen of what I thought were really great ideas for lists and syndromes and even clever chapter titles ("Adverbs My Ass," "Get a Spell-Checker, Buddy," "Are You Talking to Me!") but I hit a wall. You see, every time I wrote down what I thought was an actual useful rule, there was, like, immediately right there in my head, fifteen exceptions to that rule, and I thought to myself, *Dave, this is like a really truly genuinely bad thing for a business which more or less prides itself on seeing the world as black and white.* To my bed I took; lost and filled with a hopeless despair. I awake now: older and—yes!—wiser, but all the same still resolved to share my hard-earned wisdom with those who toil in our wake. My children: It's all relative, you make it up as you go along, rules are for fools, honor thy mother and father, do your own thing, write what you know, avoid flashbacks, and make it new.

Oh, and punctuation is an art, not a science. 🍎

David Haynes

David Haynes has been recognized by *Granta* as one of America's best young novelists. The author of six critically acclaimed novels and five children's books, he is director of creative writing at Southern Methodist University in Dallas, Texas. The former sixth grade teacher's short stories have been heard on Selected Shorts on NPR, and his novels have been recognized by the American Library Association.

Don't Tell It Like It Is

by Deb Olin Unferth

Who says fiction is like life? That art imitates experience? That narrative is naturally empathetic? Fiction is not natural. It imitates nothing but itself. More than resembling what we see, it expresses what is absent, what we dimly desire. Fiction is everything that life is not.

The external world is not like fiction. In real life we repeat ourselves—day in and out, year upon year. We sit beside our lovers and say the same endearments or curses, make the same confessions, tell the same stories whether the face before us changes or not. We walk down hallways, make phone calls, answer them, saying, *hello, hello, hello, how are you, how are you, you wouldn't believe what happened yesterday, this morning, last night* .... We walk the same streets, visit the same desks or others like them. Our clocks, our steps, our very heartbeats follow the same pattern. In fiction such repetition would be disastrous, like a gibbering idiot's scrawl, the same sentences over and over and over. Of course, there are precedents for it: Gertrude Stein, the Bible, but is that any excuse?

The internal world is not like fiction. In real life, the inside of the mind is, frankly, a mess. It's a chaotic swampland of shady motivations, strange guilts and joys, incomprehensible connections. When one writes "Y thought, 'X,'" the writer is identifying only a single thread in a hypothetical mind tangle, isolating one random stick in the stack. Think

We don't have revelations that we learn from. … Or we have no revelation, we continue down our partly lit paths unwatched, unknown even to ourselves. In fiction, pretend otherwise.

of all the thoughts you have at any given moment. Fiction, in comparison, is flat as cardboard. It is not the funhouse mirror of experience. It is the tea-cup ride, the orderly line, the functional bank machine standing inexplicably on the corner in the heaviest war zone. Writerly claims to record the stream of consciousness are rubbish. The layers of thought and image (and whatever else is in there) that whiz by and spin off in six seconds would require

a volume of explanation, and even if each idea compressed in that short period could be represented, the experience of fluidity and brevity would be lost in the time it took to read it through—not to mention that we'd have to take into account all the thoughts the reader would be having in the meantime, thereby wrecking any salvaged similarity to the original. The closest writing comes to imitating the raging speed and creativity of thought associa-

tions jumping in the mind like synapses is the simile—a paltry few words here and there,

hardly a rendition. No, it's impossible to create anything like accurate representation. Don't try. Dumb it down. Give us the crippled version. Lie.

The meaning of our lives is not like fiction. The narrative we live makes little sense no matter how hard we try to slide it into slots we are much more familiar with: the fairy tale, the novel, the Kleenex commercial. And despite our efforts to line it up, label it, cut or fold it to fit, real life is not like the alphabet, the encyclopedia, the phone bill. It doesn't fall into easy categories. Rewards don't come when we deserve them; sometimes they come when we don't—haphazardly, falling out of the sky like bricks or TV sets or rain. Adventures are rare, morals accidental, conversations wordy. Coincidences are usually uninteresting, not amazing, not un/lucky. We don't have revelations that we learn from. We have revelation after revelation, shining, hallucinatory, or dull-plated, silvery, and still we make the same bad and good choices for the same bad and good reasons. Or we have no revelation, we continue down our partly lit paths unwatched, unknown even to ourselves. In fiction, pretend otherwise. Have your characters make meaningful choices with corresponding consequences. For God's sake, don't make it like it is. We've had enough of that horror.

Unless … you want to write something *really* interesting. In that case, tell it like it is. Embrace the mimetic fallacy. Write the slow walk to the water fountain. Describe the refrigerator. Record each time you see your shoe. There it is again. There it is again. And again. And again. And again. ❦

Deb Olin Unferth

A professor of English at the University of Kansas, Deb Olin Unferth's work has appeared in *Harper's*, *Conjunctions*, *StoryQuarterly*, NOON, *Fence*, *3rd Bed*, and other publications. She received a Pushcart Prize and a fellowship from the Illinois Arts Council. She is a founder and editor of *Parakeet* and has an MFA in fiction from Syracuse.

Plucking Your Character's Eyebrows

by Thisbe Nissen

When my boyfriend first read a full draft of my most recent novel (a draft which, I'll note, a number of friends and editors had already been through) he started circling eyebrows. As it turned out, I have a terrible tic. Or rather, my characters, one and all, have a terrible tic: They can't stop raising their eyebrows. It's kind of mortifying to have someone point out that this novel, which you claim to have already gone over with a fine-tooth comb, literally has someone on every other page raising his or her eyebrows. How could that have escaped all censor? Is the raising of eyebrows so ubiquitous in my life that I don't even note it? God love Word's "Find" function! Find what: eyebrow. And so I got to plucking.

Now, you can't help, while you're plucking, but to give those brows a good hard study, try to understand how on earth you could have let them get so bushy, why on earth no one's pointed you straight for the waxing salon. Seems to me eyebrow-raising might be the *like* of the dramatization vocabulary. You know, like, everyone does it, but it's, like, not totally noticeable, since, like, *everyone's* doing it, unless you're, like, doing it, like, *all* the time, so it's like you can't even, like, hear, like, what someone's, like, trying to, like, say, like you know?

There's a potentially sympathetic defense for the *like*-ers, isn't there? The phenomenon stems from insecurity, from the fear of actually making a statement, of claiming your own words as definitive. If you *like* before and after everything you say, no one can accuse you of self-righteousness, or pomposity (or of speaking English, for that matter). *Like*, in the most generous of defenses, might be considered a symptom of humility.

The compulsive raising of eyebrows does not make for interesting or insightful fiction. It's ultimately about as observant as noting when a character breathes or blinks.

And so, in my own defense of eyebrow-raising, let me posit that I think it's well-intentioned, if ultimately unsuccessful and profoundly annoying. I think it comes from an attempt to heed the *show, don't tell* doctrine. I think I'm making pathetic stabs at subtlety. I think I've got people raising their eyebrows willy-nilly in an effort *not* to break a whole bunch of *other* rules of thumb. I'm avoiding the dreaded adverbial modifier ("she said, skeptically") and trying to dramatize rather than exposit, to let physical action stand in for lengthy, boring description ("He wondered if she was telling the truth, and his facial expression reflected that underlying suspicion"). In my further defense, I might also be doing what fiction writers are encouraged to do when writing dramatic scenes: to watch the characters, see what they're doing, listen to what they're saying. I'm listening and I'm watching, and these people just raise their eyebrows a hell of a lot! Which is maybe indicative of my characters being generally questioning souls, inquisitive, searching, curious, unwilling to settle for easy answers, unwilling to accept superficial explanations. Or maybe it's, like, more indicative, of, like, maybe, like, me just not trying very hard, you know?

Regardless of possible defenses, this much is certain: The compulsive raising of eyebrows does not make for interesting or insightful fiction. It's ultimately about as observant as noting when a character breathes, or blinks, and that's not to say there's no room for breathing and blinking in fiction, for certainly there are moments when the breath and the blink can serve purposes beyond their obvious and autonomic natures. Likewise, I'd say, the eyebrow raise.

And so, yes, I pluck. I pluck rigorously, religiously, with unre-lenting vigor and thoroughness. I'm like the airport security of eyebrow-raising; nothing gets by me anymore. I am on permanent raised-eyebrow vigil. But just let me say that you can be a judicious eyebrow plucker without winding up like one of those old ladies who's been pulling out those hairs so long she's got nothing left and has to draw hers in with an eyebrow pencil, thin arched lines in Cocoa Brown or Night Black suggesting where an eyebrow might go, if it existed. Which is all to say: Strive for ruthlessness, not baldness! After all, most people *do have* eyebrows, and sometimes—very, very occasionally—something quite important, and interesting, might be revealed through a judiciously placed and very subtle lift. ❦

Thisbe Nissen

Thisbe Nissen feels particularly derivative writing a contributor's note for a book that Michael Martone is connected to in any way, but will nonetheless take the opportunity to note that *Osprey Island* is out in paperback.

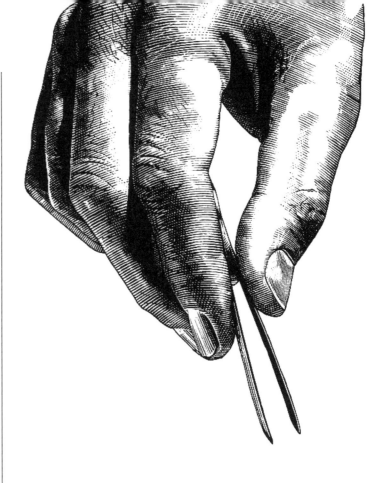

Thumbs

by Joseph Geha

He who returns an honest answer plants a kiss on the lips.

—Proverbs 24:26

Years ago when I was a fledgling writer and filled with a spirit of greenhorn humility, I searched for writerly advice from those I thought best able to provide it: writing teachers, editorial assistants, magazines devoted to the writer's trade. And all of them I found to be quite earnest in their desire to help.

The magazines, for instance. I remember one day in particular, eating lunch in the backroom of my uncle's Lebanese grocery, reading a column which flatly stated that a person must stop reading fiction once he's decided to become a fiction writer. I put down my goose liver sandwich, wiped my mouth with a corner of the apron and reread the sentence before going on. Yeah, that's what he was saying, all right. The reason? *Because you don't want to have your personal style infected by that of another writer.*

College writing teachers. I had a good one. Only one. (Which was all I really needed.) And others who were not so good. One of whom suggested that I change the emphasis of the play I was writing for his drama class, a play that dealt with the turmoil in an immigrant family headed by a headstrong, possibly deranged father. His advice: Minimize

> *When you finish reading my piece, put down this book and pick up another, your Bible. No kidding.*

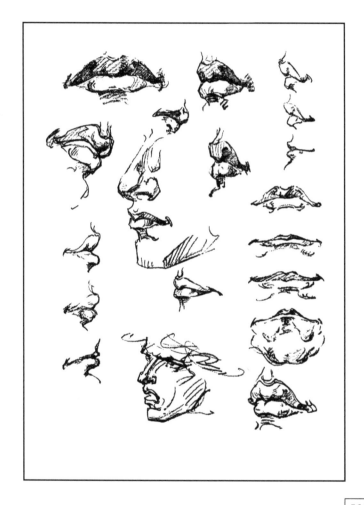

the father's scenes and insert something bigger.

Okay, like what, for instance?

His honest-to-goodness suggestion: "A computer gone wild. One that eventually portends, perhaps, nuclear annihilation?"

When I became a teacher myself, I understood that most of us mean well. That's the thing, though. Dangerous advice can come from the best-intentioned. Like my ex-wife, who suggested once that I'd improve my writing by just taking out "all that Arab stuff."

The most dangerous advice of all can come from editors and editorial assistants. What makes their suggestions so hazardous is the implication that "if you'd only change a little here, or a little there, and gosh, we'd be delighted to publish this pathetic little attempt of yours and save you from perishing for one more academic year."

Which would be fine if it worked that way. But it doesn't. See, once you get them past the standard printed rejection slip stage, editors have to write *something*. *Anything*. Words. Blah, blah. We found your story charming (or moving, or funny); however, we also found it too—whatever. They don't even *remember* what they wrote. Honest. Twenty years ago I had a courageous friend who desperately needed a publication. A highly respected literary magazine was interested in his short story, but the editor didn't like the ending and wanted it completely changed. The *ending*! He even stated that the story would be rejected otherwise. My friend gave it about a week of thought and anguish, and finally he wrote back saying he really, *really* wanted the ending to remain the way it was. The editor responded immediately: Sure, okay, no problem. The magazine published the story, exactly as the writer had written it. They even submitted it for a national award, and it took first place. True story.

Okay, so here's *my* advice. When you finish reading my piece, put down this book and pick up another, your Bible. No kidding.

My first teaching job was in a southerly Midwestern town that the English department had nicknamed the buckle of the Bible Belt, and it wasn't too long before I had handed to me a Bible of my very own. Not some street corner King James version, either. This was a New Jerusalem Bible, huge, thick, its pages dark with tiny-fonted annotations.

No stranger to the Good Book, I opened it to Proverbs and started paging through. Well, I never expected to like this newer translation. And yet, reading on, I discovered that in giving up the powerful seventeenth-century poetic tone, it had acquired—at least in Proverbs—a different kind of power, that of plain common sense. For instance:

Like a madman hurling firebrands, arrows and death, so is the man who lies to his neighbor and then says, "It was all a joke."

—Proverbs 26:18

Better open rejection than voiceless love.

—Proverbs 26:18

Do not set foot too often in your neighbor's house for fear he tires of you and comes to hate you.

—Proverbs 25:17

But the one that really surprised me, as a young man searching for advice, read as follows.

Give up listening to instruction, my son, and ignoring what knowledge has to say.

—Proverbs 19:27

Come again? Of course there was a footnote: Some scholars claimed it had to be an unfinished proverb; others considered it to be ironic. *Irony*—in the *Bible*? Well, okay, maybe. But me, I picture King Solomon sitting there and dictating one proverb after another after another after another after another ... until finally, in his wisdom, he heaves a sigh, maybe smacks the fist of one hand into the palm of the other, and comes right out and says what he'd started thinking back about maybe eight proverbs ago: *Aw screw it! Stop listening to advice while ignoring the simple truth right there in front of you!* And the scribe just goes ahead and takes it down.

The simple truth right in front of you is this: If you want to be a writer, you need to do two things. You need to read. And you need to write. That's all.

The rest is just advice. 🌱

Joseph Geha

Born in Lebanon, Joseph Geha is the author of *Through and Through: Toledo Stories* and *Holy Toledo*. His fiction has been awarded a fellowship grant from the National Endowment for the Arts, as well as inclusion in the *Pushcart Prize: Best of the Small Presses* and the Arab American Archive of the Smithsonian Institution. His work appears widely in literary magazines, anthologies, and other publications, including *The Iowa Review*, *Denver Quarterly*, *The New York Times*, and *Epoch*. He is a recently retired creative writing professor at Iowa State University.

Don't Break That POV, Hand Me the Pliers

by Jay Brandon

The friend who was criticizing my short story said, "You can't do that!"

"I can't? Can't do what?"

"You changed points of view. You can't do that. There's a rule."

And? I thought. *Are the fiction police going to arrest me?*

I had broken the rule quite deliberately. I was writing the story in third person precisely so that I could change points of view. But this was forbidden, my friend explained, because I was writing *close third*, showing a character's thoughts. You can only do that with one character.

I don't know who invented this rule, or why. My friend's opinion was a small matter to me, but unfortunately my editor knew this rule as well. All right, in one novel I had a scene late in the book of the villain talking to his girlfriend, and I had never shown them alone together previously. Can't break point of view, my editor said. So I wrote a couple of other scenes from the villain's point of view to go earlier in the book. That somehow made it okay.

You must know the rules, because if you don't, someone else will. He or she will be teaching them to you, destroying the illusion that you are professional equals.

The current compromise between my editor and me is that I can shift points of view within a

As far as I'm concerned, the only rule of fiction is that you must hold the reader's interest.

scene, but I have to put in a line break first, thus:

Such a break usually signals a passage of time or change of scene. In my case, it sometimes means I'm going to switch to a different character's point of view within the same scene. Apparently this line break throws the fiction police off your trail, and while they're standing there above the break scratching their heads, I'm free to commit another crime against fiction.

As far as I'm concerned, the only rule of fiction is that you must hold the reader's interest. But I'm not the only one concerned. You have to appease the editors and other close readers.

You must know the rules. You must be on friendly, even intimate, terms with them. That way you can take one aside some evening, slip away for a few drinks, invite the rule back to your place, and then gently and with great tenderness violate the hell out of it. 🦋

Jay Brandon

Jay Brandon has had more than a dozen novels published in as many countries, most recently *Running with the Dead*, and would have written even more except that he is also a lawyer and helping raise three children. Each of his novels takes aspects of people, places, and happenings in the world of law and adds Jay's own brand of gripping suspense.

To Hell With Likability

by Rick Moody

Humbert Humbert, the unreconstructed pedophile. Likeable? Hell, no! Raskolnikov, who murders his landlady for no particular reason. Likeable? Hell, no! Hamlet, who cannot be bothered to avenge his father's murder for several acts and who then occasions a gigantic bloodbath: definitely a self-centered and morose prick, whose girlfriend, because of his inattention, goes nuts and winds up in a nunnery. Good guy? Not a good guy. Not at all. Henry V disavows his best friend Falstaff as soon as he assumes the throne. He weds the daughter of the king of France after slaughtering the better part of the able-bodied men of her nation, for which he never bothers to apologize. Good guy? No! Not a good guy! Rabbit Angstrom, in the Updike tetralogy, cheats on his wife during her pregnancy and, three books later, showing little improvement, sleeps with his daughter-in-law. Camus's murderer in *L'étranger*. Bad, bad, bad! What about Stephen Dedalus in *Ulysses*, the arrogant would-be intellectual who says *non serviam* to his mother on her deathbed? Likeable? Not likeable! What about Molloy in Beckett's trilogy? He spends most of his time sucking on rocks. What about any character in any book by Thomas Bernhard? What about the narrators of *Celine's Journey to the End of the Night* or *Death on the Installment Plan*? Kurtz in *Heart of Darkness*? What about Satan in *Paradise Lost*? Likeable? He condemns all of mankind to its fallen state for the rest of eternity! Yet he's the character in the poem we most care about!

There are any number of unlikeable women characters, too. Amanda Keeler in Dawn Powell's splendidly scurrilous *A Time to*

Be Born. Becky Sharpe in *Vanity Fair*. Sabbath Hawks in *Wise Blood*. Or what about Madame Bovary? She wants for even a split second of insight into her own motivation. Personally, I find Catherine Earnshaw pretty repellant in *Wuthering Heights*. And yet perhaps more often in a novel the women characters are *supposed to be likeable*, as with the scarcely to be endured Esther Summerson in *Bleak House*. It's precisely the author's unyielding belief in the sentimental perfection of feminine beauty and grace that makes Esther so dull and so forgettable. If only she had a delicate self-cutting compulsion! If only she kept a chimney sweep around for the occasional hookup! If only she were a secret lesbian or was controlling the London legal profession from behind a perfumed curtain! The same is true of Milton's Eve (and Adam, for that matter), and, for my money, a number of Henry James's feminine protagonists. I'd prefer James's vaunted psychological realism if it contained some cursing, some alcoholism, some incest, some suicide.

Despite these myriad examples (more could easily be provided), there are many reviewers and critics these days who would have you believe that an unlikeable character is somehow a *liability*. These writers, I would argue, are the hacks. These are the people who have given up loving a challenge. These are the people who don't see the novel as terrain in which learning can take place. These are the people who are determined to ensure that the novel exists as a poor cousin to the afternoon chat shows with their relentlessly heartwarming stories of overcoming adversity.

You may even have heard this particular bit of advice about your own work (*I just didn't like this character! This character just isn't sympathetic!*) from your more witless friends in writing workshops. These people,

> *If what you require is reassurance that everything you personally have done is sweet and good and worthy of admiration, I suggest you go work in greeting-card composition.*

and my apologies for saying it somewhat stridently, *should be ignored at all costs*. Fiction's purpose is not gentle affirmation of life! If what you are looking for is gentle affirmations that make undeniable the validity of your particular ideological system, or if what you require is reassurance that everything you personally have done is sweet and good and worthy of admiration, I suggest you go work in greeting-card composition! The purpose of art is to depict life as it *is*, or as it *will be*, whether in the sphere of human drama or in the strange, ominous vault of the human imagination. The purpose of art is to depict actual human psychology, not some idealized version thereof. Literature, at its best, gives voice to the voiceless, to the preterites, because, I figure, the successes, or what passes for them these days, get to be in the newspaper every day. They get to make a lot of money and to worry about the dullest stuff, like the quantity of crabgrass in their lawn.

The purpose of art is truth, and the truth, as regards the human condition, is that humans are complex, neither all good nor all bad, neither all courageous nor all cowardly, neither all yearning nor all chilly, and there is no perfect shapeliness to their lives. Humans die for no reason, or they fail to thrive after promising beginnings. The humans who are the most loathsome, the most unyielding and cruel to their friends and families, often excel in the world, destroying a lot of ethically minded types along the way. The heroes secretly shoot their veins full of steroids so they can hit more home runs. And the really philanthropic failures, the ones who save a hundred thousand dollars from their job at the dry cleaner in order to give all this money to the orphanage, are sometimes robbed at gunpoint, never to recover from the trauma.

Ergo: Never ever ever ever ever ever ever ever ever ever ever ever ever ever ever ever

worry if your character is *likeable* or *sympathetic*. People who want only characters who are affirmations of some timid notion of "sympathetic" psychology are actually contemptuous of most of the rest of us. They are the people who secretly *hate* people, who hate the pocked skin, the stammer, the fits of rage, the compulsive masturbation, though these are pandemic in the real world. Paris Hilton probably prefers sympathetic characters, assuming she is able to read. Flee from all readers who tell you that your character is just too dark or too miserable or that no one's going to want to read about him or her. Worry, instead, about

whether your character is *true*, and by this I don't mean that your character talks exactly the way a sixteen-year-old would talk, or that your character behaves exactly like all other white Anglo-Saxon Protestants, or whomever. Worry about whether your character is complex in the way that life is complex and bittersweet. It will take us a while to figure out who this person is, what he or she stands for, but then, just maybe, we will love your character despite his or her faults, just the way we feel about the actual people we know. Those are the characters you want, the ones that require a little effort to love. The prodigals. ❧

Rick Moody

Rick Moody's most recent novel is *The Diviners*. He is also the author of *Demonology*, *Purple America*, *The Ring of Brightest Angels Around Heaven*, *The Ice Storm* and *Garden State*, which won the Pushcart Press Editors' Book Award. He is a past recipient of the Addison Metcalf Award and a Guggenheim fellowship. Moody has contributed fiction and essays to most major publications and has been widely anthologized. He lives in New York.

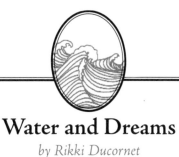

Water and Dreams

by Rikki Ducornet

My first four novels are ruled by the elements: earth, fire, water, and air. These books are informed by and much indebted to the French philosopher Gaston Bachelard—his gentle manias and irresistible investigations into the nature of the imagining mind.

Water's book, *The Fountains of Neptune*, tells the story of a boy who, seduced by the vision of his drowned mother's face, tumbles into the sea. Retrieved, he is suspended in a coma that lasts for fifty years. Like a fossil Bachelard describes in *The Poetics of Space*, the boy is "asleep in [his] form", the deep waters of his precarious mind kept murmuring by his doctor in her clinic, "where water is tamed in basins, bathtubs, and wells, and where even the ironwork of the garden fences, the kiosks, and the gate, look like an abstraction of a water oily with eels."

Guided by Bachelard's *Water and Dreams*, I decided that my novel's variable music would evoke water of all kinds: swift, still, and shallow; stagnant, transparent, and frozen over; sweet, tainted, opaque. For example, when a sailor sings:

> I've been to Bûr Sa'id,
> Shāhbāzpur and Hooghly,
> Crooked Island, Easter Island;
> I've been to Corpus Christi.

I wished to evoke the bubbly turbulence in the wake of a boat pulled along by a good wind.

And the novel is punctuated by the water's *meteoric* forms (and this is a term taken from the period I evoke in the book's

How I travel is how I write my books. It is enough to have a dream for a guide, an intuition, an element.

early stages): sleet, snow, hail, rain and drizzle—all *powers*, here consciously associated in order to suggest the many moods of the sea. What fol-

lows intends to evoke both a needling rain and the heave of heavy weather.

Saturday and pissing vinegar. The old port has vanished in the rain; port and sky and sea all smeared together like a jam of oysters, pearl-grey and viscous.

I made lists that I no longer have, but looking into the novel's opening pages I find: sea, firewater, whisky, rum; ocean, sea-talkers, sailors, mermen; moonshine, shellback, dancing ships; fish, mists, listing ships; foam, sea wolf, jelly fish; floodlands, liquid amber, tears; starboard, sea worm, milky haze; hail, surf, tidewater, rain; sops, floating island, splashing, drifting ....

And I imagined a book *bathed* in light, light a sensuous medium that, like water, seeps into every crack. Chapters three and four take place in an underwater haze.

◆

The idea that the music of the text would evoke waters of various kinds was the only imposition I engaged; beyond that, as with all my books, the novel was expected to reveal itself. The characters dropped in and decided the direction the book—their book—would take. As did the unexpected collisions of words. The novel's intention evolved from within; the entire process had a weather of its own.

Bachelard says: "And the words wander away looking in the nooks and crannies of vocabulary for new company, bad company." Such bad company is scary and exhilarating—above all, subversive—as it forces the writer to question her presumptions and keeps her on her toes.

◆

I think of a novel as an unfolding landscape, an entire country waiting to be deciphered. I have always leaned into new places, tugged along by curiosity and an expanding waking dream. How I travel is how I write my books. It is enough to have a dream for a guide, an intuition, an element. "How can one not dream while

writing?" Bachelard asks. "It is the pen that dreams."

Finally, writing is a species of practical magic. Like sugar in water, the words one employs must dissolve and altogether vanish. ❧

Rikki Ducornet

Artist and fiction writer Rikki Ducornet is the author of seven novels, including *The Fan Maker's Inquisition*, a *Los Angeles Times* Book of the Year, and *The Jade Cabinet*, a finalist for the National Book Critics Circle Award. She has illustrated books by Robert Coover and Jorge Luis Borges.

I ~~ALWAYS~~

by Steve Tomasula

File name: I never for Martone.doc

1/26/05

1/23/05

12/26/04

[if you need a title, how about: I ~~ALWAYS~~

I

~~always~~

NEVER ~~mean~~

write, one ~~letter~~ word

@ a time, or change a ~~word~~ letter—

First thought best thought!—or ~~change edit~~ revise my mind,

~~constructing seducing morphing worrying arranging shaping (like~~

~~sculpting water)~~ ~~forcing inventing finding~~ imagining words for meaning, ~~plot syntax grammar syllables~~ meaning determining ~~constraining suggesting needing straight-jacketing begging demanding~~ words, ~~thought nuance shades sequence~~ words ~~constraining suggesting demanding limiting begging~~ requiring letters, ~~symbols ink characters pixels~~ letters ~~combining forging shaping embodying mimicking pantomiming~~ forming words, words ~~forming shaping deconstructing altering outlining suggesting shadowing corrupting distorting destroying multiplying narrowing~~ embodying meaning, meaning *There are no good writers* ~~only good letters determining words determining meaning~~ writing one ~~desire letter fear thought idea feeling joy emotion pain hope anguish~~ word at a time, meaning meaning ~~seeps leaks bursts blooms runs erupts seeps sneaks escapes~~

leaks bursts blooms empties
drains extrudes flies emerges
from words fixed rolling wal-
lowing mercurial mirrored frozen expressed in letters born of
plan purpose accident objective
chance appearance lead light
sound intent meaning meaning

only good rewriters and I never
always mind my revisions or
mean write one word letter @
a time,
a word-letter-meaning
ALWAYS
never
I ❦

Steve Tomasula

Steve Tomasula is the author of the novels *VAS: An Opera in Flatland, IN & OZ,* and *The Book of Portraiture.* His short fiction has appeared in *The Iowa Review, Fiction International,* and *McSweeney's.* Recent criticism and essays are included in *Musing the Mosaic, Data Made Flesh, Leonardo, New Art Examiner,* and other magazines both here and in Europe. He teaches creative writing at the University of Notre Dame.

Writing Rule No. 1

by Fern Kupfer

It seems I don't have any hard-and-fast writing rules. No superstitions. No obsessions, compulsions, absolutes. I don't have set-in-stone places or times to write. Working on a novel, I was easily called away from task: to answer the phone, to go out to lunch with a friend, to nap in a sunny room on a winter's day. I *always* stopped writing when a child came home from school. (That is why I'm probably a better mother than I am a writer.)

There's the usual: I warm up by reading something that's similar to what I'm working on. Then I read what I've written the day before. I read aloud often because you often *hear* things that you don't *see* on a page. My husband—who's a writer—always reads what I write. I take his suggestions cheerfully. I revise and revise, of course. But I'm hardly a perfectionist.

Truth is—although *having written* gives a certain pleasure—I don't much like the act of writing. I had a newspaper

> *I always stopped writing when a child came home from school. (That is why I'm probably a better mother than I am a writer.)*

column for eleven years. Writing columns is satisfying because they are short and there's a deadline. It was also fun giving my opinion instead of having to make something up. But when *Newsday* "reorganized" and I was essentially fired, I didn't miss the writing.

I enjoy writer gossip as much as the next person. Who writes in the nude? Who scribbles longhand on legal pads? Who sits nine to five at a desk, just as if he has an office job? But the quirks and quibbles of a writing life are romanticized. Some people have rules and helpful tricks. I think it's more like that Nike commercial: Just do it! ❧

Fern Kupfer

A professor of creative writing at Iowa State University, Fern Kupfer is the author of three novels and a nonfiction book, *Before and After Zachariah*, which describes her family's life with their severely handicapped child and the decision for residential placement. Her most recent novel, *Love Lies*, is a comedic mystery. Her fiction and short essays have appeared in numerous popular journals and magazines including *Parents*, *Women's Day*, *Newsweek*, *Redbook*, *Family Circle*, and *Cosmopolitan*.

Bricoleur's Mishmash

by Wendy Rawlings

I write on a desk made from an unfinished door I bought at Home Depot. It cost twenty bucks, plus the sandpaper and varnish. At artist's colonies or in hotel rooms I tried to work on proper desks and found the experience pinched, contracting. A door makes for a work-space deep and wide. Numberless times I've cleared it of clutter. But the tidiness is deafening as silence. My husband, in his studio at the other end of the house, works on a door desk as well. Sanded pale, empty as the plains but for the laptop placed equidistant from either end, my husband's desk strikes me as a testament to his heritage (100 percent Dutch Calvinist) and his writerly sensibility (his most recent book: a collection of fifty prose poems, each exactly one hundred words long).

What's on my desk right now? Precariously stacked piles of open books flanked by piles of old standbys that, though shut, must remain within easy reach. These days it's James Salter's *Light Years*, a novel I love in a way that's almost familial, and Lawrence Durrell's *Justine*, which I'm not crazy about, but which contains any number of strangely arresting, epigrammatic sentences. Here's one picked at random: "Shyness has laws: You can only give yourself tragically, to those who least understand." The stacked piles of open books are from the university library, a bricoleur's mishmash I'm using to spur me forward on a short story and an unrelated

piece of creative nonfiction. So it's William James's *Varieties of Religious Experience* bedded down with *Forgotten Elegance: The Art, Artifacts, and*

Peculiar History of Victorian and Edwardian Entertaining in America, *The Anchor Book of New American Short Stories* face down in an embrace with

my yellowed paperback *Roget's Thesaurus.*

Then there are the objects, arrayed around my iMac like offerings at a shrine: Burt's

Bee's milk and honey body lotion, a box of Kleenex, a tin of licorice Altoids, lip balm, a cloth to clean my eyeglasses, some Atomic FireBalls (the candy, not the catastrophe), a timer for when I give in to the old 90-percent-perspiration adage and do a series of writer's fartleks—five minutes writing madly, five staring into space. Finally, a magnificent sectional tray containing black licorice from Australia, the Netherlands, Germany, and Finland. I would prefer booze and cigarettes, but I make an unconvincing Dorothy Parker.

In Vivian Gornick's memoir, *Fierce Attachments*, I came across a description of Bronx

tenement life in the 1940s: "the women calling out to each other, the sounds of their voices mixed with the smell of clothes drying in the sun, all that texture and color swaying in open space."

I couldn't render the sense of the way matter needs to accrue around me when I write any better than that. Is it that I'm a Jew and a prose writer? I think of both my heritage and genre as prone to messiness, energetic disarray. How else, except amid chaos, to get anything done? 🌱

Wendy Rawlings

A professor at the University of Alabama, Wendy Rawlings received her PhD in creative writing from the University of Utah in 2000. The recipient of residency fellowships from The MacDowell Colony, Virginia Center for the Creative Arts, and Yaddo, Rawlings was awarded the John Farrar Fellowship in Fiction at the Bread Loaf Writers' Conference. A collection of her short stories, *Come Back Irish*, won the 2000 Sandstone Prize for Short Fiction. Her work has appeared in *Tin House*, *Fourth Genre*, *Bellingham Review*, and *The Atlantic Monthly*.

Knock Knock Knock

by Samantha Hunt

Sometimes, if I'm lucky, I'll wake up in the middle of the night with a phrase or sentence echoing in my head. I have never felt responsible for these words plucked from an unconscious reservoir, but rather imagine that they have arrived here, in the dead of night, from some exterior source, possibly even off the lips of someone I was talking to in a dream. The phrases rarely make sense. "You weren't going to do all that you nosy queen of habitat," I remember one of them saying.

Despite the lack of meaning gleaned from the phrases, I feel that to ignore these words would show a terrific lack of respect for mystery, and so it is my one writing rule that I force myself to get up in the wee hours and record these (really often very dumb) messages so that I might remember them in the morning. "Into the forest I walk with the good bear. Goodbyes and lacerations." What the hell does that mean? I haven't the slightest idea, but I wrote it down anyway. It's the rule.

Perhaps these phrases are the lowliest of words, the desperate beggars that come knocking at midnight, wanting to be put to use in a story. Maybe they are ghost phrases destined to wander in ambiguity until some mortal tries to make sense of them. Or perhaps they are stern warnings that I am just too dense to decode. Or else maybe they are gifts, gifts of nonsense. It doesn't seem to matter. All I know is that were I to ignore these foolish words I would somehow cheapen the value of all words. So in the dark I obey these voices, these midnight inconveniences, not out of superstition but because they connect me to that which is most crucial to my writing: the gloriously inadvertent, the perfectly unintended.

Samantha Hunt

Samantha Hunt is a writer and artist from New York; her novel is called *The Seas*. She teaches writing and editing at Pratt Institute and is the fiction editor of *Crowd* magazine.

Use a *Dying Fall* in Every Work, But Not Too Often

by Ed Skoog

In Shakespeare's *Twelfth Night*, Duke Orsino pleads:

> If music be the food of love, play on,
> Give me excess of it; that surfeiting,
> The appetite may sicken, and so die.
> That strain again, it had a dying fall;
> O, it came o'er my ear like the sweet sound
> That breathes upon a bank of violets,
> Stealing and giving odor.

I've always liked this daisy-chain analogy: food = love = music, with the synesthetic add-on of melody's odor. To this figuration I would add the sentence, particularly the conclusion of the sentence.

Fiction, like poetry and music, should be responsive to the ear and its strange needs. To be pleased, to be surprised, and not to be hurt: These are part of the care and feeding of the reader's ear, an organ that must be nurtured and caressed to get any response. The sound of a sentence is the ultimate effect of its style, and therefore a sentence should sound interesting, following the axioms recounted by Ford Madox Ford in *Joseph Conrad: A Personal Remembrance*: "The first business of Style is to make work interesting; the second business of Style is to make work interesting; the third business of Style is to make work interesting."

Like a line of melody, like the strain that Duke Orsino hears, a sentence is above all a musical phrase and ought to obey the strict demands placed on a musician playing a score: to be calculated and

When transposed from music to prose, the term dying fall gains a number of meanings, I am told, and I try to apply all of them, as appropriate to my ear.

imaginative simultaneously, to hit not only the right *note* but the right *tone* (pay attention to the anagrams there), the meaningful timbre and the resonant value.

"Rhythm and sound," you say. "No duh. I know that you're supposed to balance long and short sentences; they taught me that in basic composition, in which I earned an A."

Correct.

But as you move in your reading from, say, Hemingway to Turgenev to Paula Fox, you'll notice specific sonic patterns popping up; you'll notice these same patterns in the Schubert assignment for next career—the sentence that doesn't seem to conclude but more accurately, like chocolate in a double boiler, melts: the dying fall.

When transposed from music to prose, the term *dying*

fall gains a number of meanings, I am told, and I try to apply all of them, as appropriate to my ear. The ends of sentences, paragraphs, and whole stories and novels may die away. My favorite paragraph in recent fiction ends with one: Philip Roth's "getting people wrong" paragraph in *American Pastoral*:

> The fact remains that getting people right is not what living is all about anyway. It's getting them wrong that is living, getting them wrong and then, on careful reconsideration, getting them wrong again. That's how we know we're alive: we're wrong. Maybe the best thing would be to forget about being right or wrong about people and just go along for the ride. But if you can do that—well, lucky you.

Going further, to end a story or a novel on a dying fall can be effective, and a bit cruel. "He has just received the cross of the Legion of Honor," the last sentence of *Madame Bovary*, does not as a sentence fall, but in the analogous music of the novel's composition, this last note is a major shift—literally, into the present tense, and figuratively, from tragedy to trivia. Similarly, the conclusion of Anton Chekhov's story "Gooseberries" shifts from fourth gear into first in a few notes, a trick that still unsettles me deeply.

> Ivan Ivanovitch undressed in silence and got into bed.
>
> "Lord forgive us sinners!" he said, and put his head under the quilt.

His pipe lying on the table smelt strongly of stale tobacco, and Burkin could not sleep for a long while, and kept wondering where the oppressive smell came from.

The rain was pattering on the window-panes all night.

Conrad and Ford also agree that a reader's interest is maintained by a continuum of "tiny, unobservable surprises," and two dying falls in a row would be large, observable, and unsurprising. My first drafts—always longhand—tend toward the embarrassingly sweeping sentence, like I'm trying to impress Molière. In revision I try to replace that enthusiasm (a mode that I'm equally suspicious of in music and food and love) with coldness (which I don't enjoy in music or food or love) and hope that the two forces find equilibrium in later drafts. I try to allow a dying fall to survive, and rise, every few pages. The dying fall is one of thousands of terms for how music works; what I have found is that an attention to this kind of sound has attuned my ear to other sounds at the ends of sentences, it seems, in some small habit, like a mouse scuttling out of the kitchen at dawn. ❦

Ed Skoog

Ed Skoog's poems have appeared in *Poetry* and *The New Republic*, among many others. He lives in California.

Cramming

by Erin McGraw

*R*ule of thumb. Already we're in trouble. It's the nature of art to resist rules, and no sooner do we create one than we come across a gorgeous exception. Interior movement should be balanced by external action—unless you're Virginia Woolf. War stories will not have cross-gender appeal—unless you're Erich Maria Remarque. Ditto love stories, unless you're Jane Austen. A man I know set up his computer to alert him in red every time he typed an adverb, so passionately did he oppose modifiers in the predicate. He almost had a coronary when he read Flaubert.

We do well to hold this idea of *rule* pretty lightly, at least in what we're willing to admit in public. What we hold in secret is a whole other story. To write fiction is to enter a vast swamp bordered with superstitions, habits, and hard-won insights about the way stories

work, all of which are fancy synonyms for *rules*. A lot of them carry over from Composition 101: Vary sentence structure. Watch out for relative pronouns without clear antecedents. Avoid obfuscation.

I cram my scenes. I cram them on purpose, like a competitive eater desperately stuffing hot dogs in his mouth.

The really secret ones are so secret, at least for me, that I scarcely even admit them to myself, so I confess this with trepidation: I cram my scenes. I cram them on purpose, like a competitive eater desperately stuffing hot dogs in his mouth. If a scene is adequately doing its work with two characters, I put in a third. If I start with three, I haul in a fourth and fifth. Rarely can I get out of a piece of fiction without somebody throwing a party, either a spur-of-the-moment event or the kind with invitations and punch, because the number of characters at a party is limited only by the size of the room.

I conceive of scenes like billiards games—in particular, billiards as experienced by onlookers. While there is pleasure in watching a cleanly executed single shot, the cue tapping the striped ball just enough to tuck it into the pocket, there is more excitement generated if several balls are in play. A single angled shot—say, three to the corner—is nice, but two angles working off each other—three to the corner banks five in the side—is thrilling. Fiction works in just the same way. Two characters talking, perhaps while climbing a rock face, are interesting. They might argue, and they might flirt. One character can slip, the other can catch him, or not.

Introduce a third character, and suddenly more options exist. One character can talk, one slip, the third spot a bear not far away. The flirtation that was interesting between two characters becomes explosive between three. Instead of sliding back and forth on a predictable continuum, power divided between three characters can tilt and shift, alliances can change, and dialogue will almost necessarily be broken out of a rut. In terms of narrative structure, Pythagoras was right on the money when he demonstrated the limitations of two dimensions as opposed to three.

TAKE PARTICULAR NOTICE.

226

With this in mind, I scrutinize my scenes. If only two characters can be involved—perhaps they are on a desert island—I look for ways to bring in at least the shadow of a third. Two characters might be musing over a missing friend, their dialogue drenched in the language of the missing party. In a more populous scene, I try to make sure every character is both true to his own trajectory and has an effect on the others around him. As the action gets more complex, my operative metaphor shifts from billiards to the Mozart of *The Magic Flute*, with all the characters singing their individual motifs for everything they're worth.

When my secret rule works at its best, the scene will emerge with some of Mozart's richness, his heady, glorious pattern of melody meshing with and commenting on more melody. I like to think that if we could just get enough distance, this is exactly what humanity would sound like, so distinct and harmonious. This is an optimistic vision, I know.

Still, it's a vision that carries me forward, particularly when I'm in the grip of a rule that is by no means labor-saving. Keeping all those characters in plausible action requires lots of drafts and lots of chaos, with no promise of ever getting to the hoped-for harmony. I have the drafts of failed scenes to prove it. But scenes with only two characters feel skimpy to me now, and the only option I see is to go the other way—cramming scenes with all the life I can imagine, and then looking for more. Stuffing them in. Gorging the scene. ❦

Erin McGraw

Erin McGraw teaches writing and literature at Ohio State University and is the author of four books of fiction, including the story collections *Lies of the Saints*, *The Baby Tree*, and *The Good Life*. *Lies of the Saints* was selected as a *New York Times* Notable Book, and her work has been featured on NPR's Selected Shorts.

The Thirty-Nine Steps: A Story Writing Primer

by Frederick Barthelme

1. Step one in the great enterprise of a new and preferable you in the house of fiction is: Mean less. That is, don't mean so much. Make up a story, screw around with it, paste junk on it, needle the characters, make them say queer stuff, go bad places, insert new people at inopportune moments, do some drive-bys. Make it up, please.

2. Don't let it make too much sense.

3. Do use stuff that you care about when you're making it up. If you're mad at your mother, husband, boyfriend, wife, lover, neighbor, dog—take it out on a mother, husband, etc. and put it in the mouth of one of your characters. If you're full of love for the sea, say something nice about the bath.

4. Leaven the piece with some merchandise (figurative) you don't particularly care about but that seems to you odd, intriguing, curious, baffling, quirky. Attach this material to your characters.

5. Do not use the above to rationalize disconnected, ersatz, or unrelated oddball debris. "I'd like to talk to you but there's a giant in my room" isn't the answer to any narrative question.

6. Long plot explanations aren't going to get it. Like, when something neat (horrible?) happened to one of the characters a real long time ago, and you really really want to tell us about it, you know? Don't.

7. It doesn't particularly matter which characters these things you care about (see item 3) get attached to (these are things like pieces of dialogue, bits of description, some gesture, a look somebody gives somebody, a setting, tabletops). In fact, you're probably better off if

the stuff attaches itself in unexpected ways to wrong characters (so you don't go meaning too much, see item 1).

8. Remember: Many things have happened that, to the untrained eye, appear interesting.

9. Grace Slick. (This item updates automatically.)

10. At every turn, ask yourself if you're being gullible, dopey, pretentious, cloying, adolescent, Neanderthal, routine, dull, smarty-pants, clever, arty, etc. You don't want to be being these things.

11. Be sure there's a plot for the reader to grasp; while not necessarily the center of the story, it's key to lulling the reader into that comfort zone

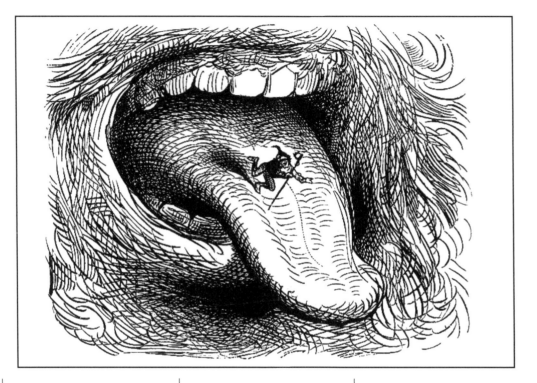

where he or she is vulnerable.

12. We can't care about sand mutants; if you do, or think you do, kill yourself.

13. Coherence is a big part of the game. Make sure the story is coherent, that the scenes flow each from the last, that the reader has the clearest sense at all times of what is going on. Err on the side of clumsiness to start with; back away later.

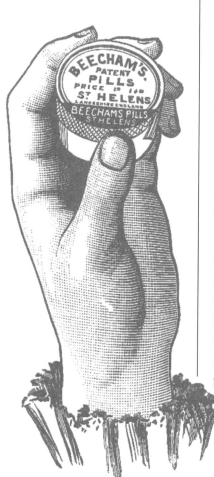

14. For dramatic purposes, you're probably well-served sticking close to an objective narrative (first-person unvoiced or third-person objective—in either case, the camera view). This forces you to write scenes in which characters do and say things to/with/for each other; these things will then construct the story for you. This expedient blocks the *telling* problem.

15. Organize the story's structure around the simplest available strategy. For example, if there's no obliging reason that the story be told in flashbacks, don't use flashbacks. Don't use flashbacks simply because you get

Flashbacks, dream sequences, drug-induced beatific appreciations, Mongol hordes, etc. are not good excuses for lumbering attempts at the high rhetorical bar.

to a certain point and then think of something that requires telling in flashback if it is to be told at that point. Instead, return to the front of the story and add the material in its appropriate spot.

16. Plain chronological storytelling is a good idea. Rules on deviations: (a) avoid disruptions in time as much as possible; (b) flashbacks (and similar) are ten times more confusing to the reader than they seem to you (keep in mind for use in strategically confusing parts); (c) flashbacks, dream sequences, drug-induced beatific appreciations, Mongol hordes, etc. are not good excuses for lumbering attempts at the high rhetorical bar; (d) deviations from a norm tend to draw attention away from the story, away from the characters, away

from the emotional/spiritual center of things; (e) sometimes you may want to do this.

16½. In the redundancy department: Give us as much of the ground situation as you can as soon as possible. The first paragraph is not too soon. The first page is not too soon. Tell us who, what, when, where, etc.

17. Do not do this "artfully."

18. Remember that you want something to change over the course of the story. Something big and visible to the reader. Start with one situation and end with a clearly different situation. In between, tell us how you got from the one to the other. Don't be subtle designing this change—for purposes of nailing dramatic structure, be as reductive as humanly possible.

19. Remember this simplified structure is not the story, but the hanger on which the story hangs. The story is shirts and jackets, ribbons, the perfumes of the closet, details, bits of persuasion, rubber gunk underfoot, attitudes, hints, suggestions—everything you can attach to this hanger.

20. Obviously, these carefully hewn thirty-nine steps must be adapted to your way of working. If you're murky, then take these as bible and pare away. If you work bare bones, then murk up what you do. Throw stuff in. Make a mess. Don't clean up.

21. If you write a sentence that isn't poignant, touching, funny, intriguing, inviting, etc., take it out before you finish the work. Don't just leave it there. Don't let anyone see it.

22. To repeat, there is no place for rubbish and slop in the highly modern world of today's fiction. Every sentence must pay, must somehow thrill. Every one.

23. Also: Obscurity is not subtlety; intentional obscurity is pinheaded and unkind.

24. Doing odd stuff is good, especially, like, when you make characters do it in the story, like when stuff is happening to them and they just do this unexpected, even inappropriate stuff, and then somehow it makes a little sense. This fills the heart.

25. Don't let too many paragraphs go by without sensory information, something that can be felt, smelt, touched, tasted. Two or three paragraphs without same is too many.

26. Don't be enamored of the idea you start with, or the idea that comes to you after you've been working on a piece for a time. If you're lucky, the idea will keep changing as you write the story.

27. Don't reject interesting stuff (things for characters to say and do, things to see, places to be, etc.) because the stuff doesn't conform to your idea. Change your idea to wrap around whatever comes up.

28. If you have a story in mind to start with, leave it there. Ditto a character.

29. Apropos the big issues, note that parents don't sit around getting heartbroken about abortion; they get heartbroken because they killed the baby.

30. Or because the baby was born with fins for hands. It's the particular.

31. Sometimes it's useful to shut your eyes and imagine a scene as if it were in a movie; this helps flatten things and helps you "see" what the scene looks like.

32. Also, when doing the above, notice the things you notice in your own "real" life—like what's at the horizon; how the sun is in the sky; what kind of light's going on; the way the street, ground, grass, dirt looks; your interest in bushes; what's happening at the edges of things; buildings and signs and cars; the sounds of stuff going on around the scene. Who's that wheezing? What's that rattle? Are those leaves preparing to rustle? Etc.

33. No characters named Brooke or Amber.

34–39. Study items 1, 7, 13, 16½, and 24. ❧

Frederick Barthelme

An artist, educator, editor, and writer, Frederick Barthelme is well known for his fiction and considered a master of literary minimalism. His stories are set in the modern American South, where he was born and spent most of his life.

Barthelme studied writing at Johns Hopkins University, then began teaching at the University of Southern Mississippi, where he still teaches and where he edits the *Mississippi Review*. His books include *Elroy Nights*, *The Law of Averages*, *Moon Deluxe*, and *Double Down: Reflections on Gambling and Loss* in collaboration with Steven Barthelme.

Throw Up, Then Clean Up

by Will Allison

I am a slow writer.

For instance, it took me a long time to come up with that opening sentence, and it's not even good. Does it mean I write slowly, or I'm a writer who's slow?

I write slowly. It takes me months to finish a short story. I've been working on the same collection off and on for ten years. That I write so slowly makes me feel like a writer who's slow.

Part of the problem is that I usually don't know what I want to say until I start writing it down, which makes for a lot of trial and error. To get my head around a story—to really understand what it's about—is a glacial endeavor. I figure there's not much I can do

For me, revision is the most satisfying aspect of writing and the most seductive form of procrastination.

about this except keep writing and hope I get better.

But another part of the problem is (or was) my writing "process." I've always hated writing first drafts. First drafts are messy garbage, and writing one means acknowledging that the story on the page isn't and probably never will be as good as the one in my head, the idea of the story. It also involves making decisions about what will or will not happen in a story—walling off its many other dramatic possibilities—and in this way, writing a first draft has always felt to me a little like killing the story.

But of course a story in your head is worthless until you write it down so other people can read it. Knowing this didn't stop me from

tive—forging ahead with the first draft—offers only the prospect of more embarrassing, depressing dreck.

Not surprisingly, by the time I finally finished a first draft, I'd often lost sight of what inspired me to write the story in the first place. And then, as I'd look back over the manuscript, it would be clear I'd spent countless hours polishing and repolishing stuff that wouldn't even make the second draft.

I knew I had a problem, but I couldn't bring myself to do anything about it until, one summer, I overheard an author at the Community of Writers in Squaw Valley quoting an-

fighting first drafts, though. If I wrote a new scene one day, I was likely to spend the next several days reworking that scene again and again, because I knew that if I revised enough, I'd eventually come up with a sentence or passage I liked. For me, revision is the most satisfying aspect of writing and the most seductive form of procrastination. The alterna-

other author's prescription for writing first drafts: "Throw up, then clean up." That little piece of advice really hit home. Why clean up throw up if you're only going to throw up some more? Why try revising a story when you have only part of it to work with? So that became my rule of thumb: Throw up, then clean up. No revising until the first draft is finished. No revising until the whole story, however flawed and wretched, is on the page.

Of course, the boundary between writing and revising is like a line drawn in water. We revise (if only in our heads) even as we write something for the first time. But it's the mindset that matters. I'm still a slow writer, and I still find myself revising as I go, but now I'm much more conscious of pushing ahead. Doing so involves a high level of uncertainty and chaos—not to mention a low level of satisfaction—but at least I know that once the first draft is done and I start revising in earnest, I'll proceed more purposefully and, in the long run, a little less slowly. 🐛

Will Allison

Will Allison is a staff member at the Squaw Valley Community of Writers and teaches creative writing at Indiana University-Purdue University at Indianapolis. His short stories have appeared in *Zoetrope: All-Story*, *Kenyon Review*, *One Story*, *Shenandoah*, and many other publications.

Index

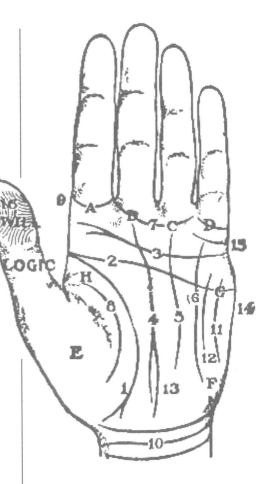

About the
Editors

MICHAEL MARTONE

Michael Martone's new book, *Michael Martone*, is a memoir made up of contributors' notes published in the contributors' notes sections of magazines. He is the author of *Unconventions*, a book of writings on writing. He directs the program in creative writing at the University of Alabama and has taught at Iowa State University, Harvard University, Syracuse University, and the Warren Wilson MFA Program for Writers.

SUSAN NEVILLE

Susan Neville is the author of four works of creative nonfiction: *Indiana Winter*; *Fabrication: Essays on Making Things and Making Meaning*; *Twilight in Arcadia*; and *Iconography: A Writer's Meditation*. Her prize-winning collections of short fiction include *In the House of Blue Lights*, winner of the Richard Sullivan prize, and *Invention of Flight*, winner of the Flannery O'Connor Award for Short Fiction. Her stories have appeared in the Pushcart Prize anthology, *Extreme Fiction* (Longman), and *The Story Behind the Story* (Norton). She lives in Indianapolis with her husband and two children and teaches writing at Butler University and in the Warren Wilson MFA Program for Writers.